ENGLISH ⊞ HERITAGE

Book of
Industrial
England

Michael Stratton and Barrie Trinder

B. T. Batsford / English Heritage
London

© Michael Stratton & Barrie Trinder 1997

First published 1997

Typeset by Bernard Cavender Design & Greenwood Graphics Publishing
Printed and bound in Great Britain by The Bath Press, Bath

Published by B.T. Batsford Ltd
583 Fulham Road, London SW6 5BY

A CIP catalogue record for this book is
available from the British Library

ISBN 0 7134 7563 3 (limp)

(Front cover) Battersea power station, London
(© British Tourist Authority Photo Library)

ENGLISH HERITAGE

Book of

Industrial England

Contents

Illustrations

Colour plates

Acknowledgements

This book is based on fourteen years of collaboration in research and postgraduate teaching in Industrial Archaeology. We acknowledge with pleasure the insights and knowledge we gained at Ironbridge from more than 200 students from many countries. We are grateful to have been able to use research by the following: Donald Payne on Dudley Wood, Paul Collins on Lye, Robert Brooks on Saddleworth, Miriam McDonald on brewhouses and Richard Butterfield on Welwyn Garden City in Chapter 1, Stuart Shaw on aircraft factories and Shane Gould on Vobster Breach in Chapter 3, Myfanwy Eaves on concrete in Chapter 5, Alan Goff on Kidderminster and Mark Watson on Dundee in Chapter 6, Geoffrey Norris on the Coalbrookdale Engineering Building in Chapter 4, David Worth on Fort Dunlop in Chapter 7, and Michael New on the Great West Road in Chapter 8. The completion of this book would have been impossible without the cheerfulness and secretarial skills of Janet Markland and Carol Sampson.

We have also gained much from the help and advice of Michael Bussell of Ove Arup Associates, Keith Falconer of RCHME, Ron Fitzgerald of Leeds Industrial Museum, Tony Herbert, Adrian Jarvis of Merseyside Maritime Museum, Stafford Linsley of the University of Newcastle upon Tyne, Joan Skinner, Jennifer Tann of the University of Birmingham, Robert Thorne of Alan Baxter Associates and Peter Wakelin of Cadw.

John Powell and Marilyn Higson, at the library of the Ironbridge Gorge Museum, have, as always, been appreciative of our needs and tolerant of our demands. We would also like to record our appreciation of the assistance and tranquillity provided by the staff of several other libraries. We have learned most from visiting working factories, and are grateful for the hospitality over many years of innumerable factory workers, managers and owners.

We also acknowledge our gratitude to the Royal Commission on the Historical Monuments of England, and to other organizations and individuals who have made available illustrations for the book, and to Peter Kemmis Betty, Monica Kendall and Charlotte Vickerstaff of Batsford, and Stephen Johnson of English Heritage.

MJS/BST
January 1997

Introduction

Industrial buildings are the greatest unused source for enlarging our understanding of English history. Between 1750 and 1850 new features appeared in the English landscape – textile mills, steam engines, potbanks, and canals. The growth of population accelerated and towns expanded. This was the first stage of a phenomenon which for more than a century historians have called the 'industrial revolution'. It spread in modified forms to other European countries, to Belgium, Switzerland, France and Germany and to the United States. In the last hundred years industry has developed in new directions, following examples set first in Germany and the United States, and subsequently in Japan. Many countries have now 'industrialized', and others yearn to do so. Most historians would now wish to qualify the idea of 'revolution', pointing out that Britain had a vigorous commercial economy by the end of the seventeenth century, that many goods continued to be made in small workshops without the aid of machinery long after 1850, and that any 'revolution' should be understood not as a single once-and-for-all transformation of society, but as a quickening of the rate of change.

Nevertheless the development of new forms of production and transport in Britain, which established a society based on manufactures as well as on cultivating land, represents a distinct phase in human history. We can learn about the growth of industry from the legal and financial records of manufacturers, from the writings of workers, travellers and government inspectors, from pictures and from maps, but evidence gained by studying the factories and other buildings of the period has perhaps the greatest potential for helping us to understand the aspirations and experiences of past generations of entrepreneurs and workers. *L- no buildings? dam?*

A rich legacy of monuments remains from the Industrial Revolution. In the Derwent valley in Derbyshire we can still see a succession of eighteenth-century cotton mills built by Richard Arkwright and his partners. In Manchester alone, eleven spinning mills built between 1800 and 1825 survive to be studied. In the area around Coalbrookdale it is possible to look at the remains not just of the blast furnace where iron was first smelted with coke in 1709, but also at those of more than a dozen other furnaces built before 1850. Numbers of buildings at Saddleworth, Kettering and in the Black Country testify to the importance of domestic manufactures, not just in the distant past but also in the early twentieth century. In Coventry the growth of motor-car manufacture can be traced through the huge factories of the age of mass production, and also through unspectacular workshops, small enough to suggest that making cars was sometimes a domestic industry. There are some gaps in our knowledge of industrial buildings – for instance, no good example of a horse-powered textile workshop of the late eighteenth century is known to survive – but research is identifying increasing numbers of such 'missing links'.

Industrial Archaeology, a systematized means of utilizing artefacts, images, structures, sites and landscapes in the investigation of the industrial past, has become a professional and intellectually rigorous activity during the last fifteen years. In this book we are principally concerned with *structures* (kilns, furnaces or buildings such as north-lit sheds or daylight factories) and *complexes* (manufacturing units comprised of structures of various kinds). Evidence from images, from pictures of all kinds, will be used, but only in so far as they relate to structures and sites. The book does not attempt to examine artefacts, the machines used in industry and their products or waste-products, nor to analyse the wider contexts of industrial landscapes.

Industrial Archaeology has matured over several decades and it is now possible to move on from what once seemed the natural way of examining our industrial past in a book: giving attention, sector by sector, to prime movers, transport, textiles, iron, non-ferrous metals, concluding with a hurried discussion of chemicals, glass and public utilities, and with scarcely a mention of twentieth-century manufactures. In both Europe and North America industrial archaeologists are acknowledging that the imposition of boundaries between sectors impedes our understanding. In all periods it is possible to observe interactions between different industrial activities. Bottle ovens and coal mines alike were features of the nineteenth-century landscape of the North Staffordshire Potteries. Many small rural collieries provided fuel for nearby brickworks, which had only local markets for their products. Aircraft manufacture from the 1930s has been dependent on factories which can roll and extrude aluminium sections. Motor-car factories provide markets for producers of seat coverings, instruments, rubber and plastics as well as for those who shape iron and steel. The different forms of manufacture have much in common: in their employment of prime movers, in the use of such building types as the north-lit shed and the by-pass factory, and in the provision of welfare facilities. It is therefore logical to turn away from a sector-by-

sector approach, and to ask what there is in common between an eighteenth-century silk mill, a mid-Victorian coal mine and a cosmetics factory of the 1930s.

This book focuses on some of the key issues relating to the understanding of factories and industrial complexes. In its most basic terms a factory accommodates workers, and processes which may need power. A manufacturing complex usually comprises not one building but many, and each needs to be considered if the whole is to be understood. A language is needed, distinct from that used by historians of architecture, which will aid our understanding of the design of factories and the motives of their builders. We shall consider one distinctive type of complex, the engineering works, and examine the meanings of one particular word, 'warehouse', which is confusingly applied to buildings with varied functions. The book concludes with a consideration of those 'model' factories and industrial settlements which were intended to influence future practice. References to particular industries can be traced through the index.

The classic period of the Industrial Revolution between 1750 and 1850 saw substantial changes in the primary forms of manufacture, the mining of coal, the manufacture of fabrics, the smelting of metals, the making of machines like steam engines and lathes, the production of pottery, chemicals and glass. It was in the second half of the nineteenth century that many of the things which people used every day – clothing, shoes, furniture and soap – came to be made on a large scale in factories. The new manufactures of the twentieth century – motor cars, aircraft, domestic appliances and processed food – originated in small-scale enterprises, but these industries came to be dominated by large factories, using American-inspired techniques of mass production, particularly those associated with the Quaker management consultant Frederick Winslow Taylor, the pioneer of time-and-motion study. In more recent times the size of many manufacturing plants has been reduced, as technology has developed and as production has been transferred to other parts of the world. Nevertheless we can learn as much from twentieth-century buildings about the experience of working in industry as from those of the Industrial Revolution period.

Many of the monuments of England's industrial past can be visited. There are museums which incorporate blast furnaces, textile mills, lead-dressing plants, potteries and coal mines. Other structures – watermills, steam engines and brick kilns – are maintained and interpreted by English Heritage and the National Trust. Still more historic buildings remain in use, or have been adapted to new uses. Factories can tell us more than castles or cathedrals about those aspects of our past which are unique to England. They are waiting to be explored.

1
Accommodating people

The factory, according to some interpretations of the Industrial Revolution, supplanted the home as the scene of manufactures. Yet some forms of production – the smelting of metals or the extraction of minerals – could never be carried out in domestic settings, while in others – such as textiles, clothing and the making of small metalwares – the relationship between domestic and factory production remained close and often symbiotic over a long period. In Northamptonshire towns like Kettering and Rothwell, workshops for the manufacture of boots and shoes were still being built at the ends of gardens of houses constructed in the 1880s (**1**), and domestic chainmaking shops were being constructed in the Black Country in the early twentieth century. This long-sustained

1 A shoemaker's workshop in New Street, Rothwell, dating from the third quarter of the nineteenth century. (Barrie Trinder)

association between domestic and factory production presents an opportunity – in trying to understand the buildings used for manufacturing, we can learn much by considering the common requirements of domestic and factory-based production.

In the home as in the factory the manufacturer's first need was space. In one sense the largest and most ornate textile factories, like Stanley Mill, Gloucestershire, or Saltaire Mill in Yorkshire, are no more than the evolutionary descendants of the loomshops or spinning-jenny shops, added to the homes of many domestic manufacturers in the Pennines in the eighteenth century.

Weaving at home

In any building accommodating people, whether working-space or dwelling-place, there is a need for light, access, heat and drainage. Study of buildings which were used for domestic manufactures shows how such facilities were provided. The most widely recognized architectural feature of domestic textile manufacture is a means of illumination, the long-light or weavers' window, to be seen in dwellings in the Pennines and in silkworking towns like Leek, Congleton and Macclesfield, where there were about 600 garret houses, most of them built between 1800 and 1820, of which about half remain (**2**). Garret houses were three-storey structures in brick, with the top floors, originally approached by ladders, lit by broad

3 Taylor Row, Barnsley, an early nineteenth-century terrace of cottages incorporating cellar loomshops for linen-weavers. (John Goodchild)

2 A double-fronted house with a weaver's loomshop on the second floor towers above its neighbours in Pitt Street, Macclesfield, laid out in the early nineteenth century. (Barrie Trinder)

small-paned windows. A local writer commented in 1817 that 'weavers carried everything with a high hand: if a new house was built, the upper storey was generally prepared with large windows fit for a weaver's workshop'.

Yet such windows were not essential for the practice of weaving. Cotton and linen fabrics were often woven in cellar loomshops (**3**). In Newark in the 1830s about a hundred weavers were involved in the manufacture of huckaback, a coarse form of linen. They worked in shops which were one-third underground so that the yarn could always be kept damp.

The most common provision for access in a domestic building used for manufactures was the taking-in door, often associated with a hoist or an external staircase. A 'piece' of woollen cloth,

made by a weaver, would be over 10m (33ft) long, and could be 2m (6½ft) wide. Taking-in doors which gave access to upper floors used entirely for manufacturing were installed in many houses where such fabrics were made. Provision for access, for materials, products and people, came to be essential in factories.

Home-made hardware

Many domestic-scale manufactures took place in buildings which were appendages to dwellings, not dissimilar from and sometimes coincident with the outbuildings used for household tasks like laundry-work and brewing, which were traditionally performed by women. In Lye in the Black Country, late nineteenth-century detached domestic workshops used for making large items of domestic hollowware were sometimes more spacious than the adjacent dwellings, some being up to 12m (39ft) long. A week's accumulated production of buckets, baths or coal-bunkers would traditionally be taken to the nearby galvanizing factory on a Friday afternoon.

Another type of detached domestic workshop, the chainshop of the south-western quarter of the Black Country around Cradley Heath, was built in considerable numbers after 1850 (**4**). The numbers engaged in the industry increased from less than 3000 in 1861 to over 6500 in 1911. Many were employed in factories, but chains were also manufactured in domestic workshops. The number of women workers increased from less than 600 (20 per cent of the work-force) in 1861, to over 2000 (32 per cent of the work-force) in 1911.

Domestic chainworkers' houses have been surveyed in Paint Cup Row in Dudley Wood (**5**). Four dwellings in a group of six were built between 1884 and 1904 and the two remaining houses in 1906. The houses are of two-up-two-down arrangement, but the rooms are placed side by side rather than front and back, resulting in an unusually long terrace. Each dwelling has a brewhouse/chainmaking shop, 3.3 by 4.3m (11 by 14ft), equipped with both domestic and chainmaking fixtures, a bread oven, a copper for washing, a stoneware sink drawing rain-water from a cistern under the floor, a hearth and an anvil block.

The development of the factory in England began almost two centuries before the construction of the Dudley Wood chainshops. One interpretation of the evolution of the factory would see it as a building in which manufacturing processes were concentrated, and in which power was generated for working machines. Such an interpretation might portray its development as a progression from peak to peak, regarding John Lombe's silk mill of 1721 in Derby, the first British factory (**6**), Richard Arkwright's mill at Cromford of 1771, the first water-powered cotton mill, and Charles Bage's iron-framed mill at Ditherington, Shrewsbury, of 1796–7 (see **10**) as landmarks, and Saltaire Mill of 1853 as the culmination of a distinct phase of evolution (see **colour plate 8**). The factory was, according to this hypothesis, conceived as a large, integrated and coherent

4 A four-hearth chainshop in Butcher's Lane, Cradley, Dudley, which was operated by a family called Nock for about a century and a half. Chainmaking ceased there about 1941. (Barrie Trinder)

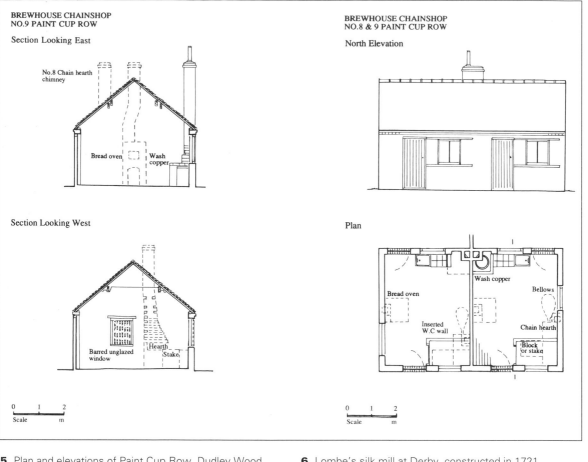

BREWHOUSE CHAINSHOP
NO.9 PAINT CUP ROW

Section Looking East

No.8 Chain hearth
chimney

Bread oven | Wash
copper

Section Looking West

Barred unglazed
window | Hearth | Stake

0   1   2
Scale   m

BREWHOUSE CHAINSHOP
NO.8 & 9 PAINT CUP ROW

North Elevation

Plan

Wash copper
Bread oven | Bellows
Inserted
W.C wall | Chain hearth
Block
or stake

0   1   2
Scale   m

5 Plan and elevations of Paint Cup Row, Dudley Wood, redrawn by Shelley White from originals by Donald Payne.

6 Lombe's silk mill at Derby, constructed in 1721. (Derby Museums)

unit, and planned accordingly. In considering the development of systems of production or the history of structural techniques, such an interpretation is valid.

Nevertheless it is possible to construct an alternative hypothesis, to see the factory as a building which develops by an evolutionary process from the working-room appended to a dwelling. Chainshops could accommodate as many as six chainmakers, as did that at Mushroom Green, Brierley Hill, or fourteen in the one preserved at Avoncroft Museum. Similarly in the textile industry a dozen or more looms, spinning-jennies or fustian-cutting frames might be accommodated in an outhouse or in an upper-storey room extending over rooms used for habitation.

Pennine loomshops

This evolutionary process is best illustrated in the Pennine parish of Saddleworth, whose centre lies 18km (11 miles) north-east of Manchester. Numerous buildings in Saddleworth provide evidence that the construction of loomshops accelerated from the 1770s and continued in the nineteenth century, and that the expansion of an essentially domestic system of manufactures occurred during the classic period of the Industrial Revolution.

Some loomshops in Saddleworth form the second floors of three-storey buildings, like the splendid example built about 1800 at New Delph (7). Others were buildings specifically designed as loomhouses which originally had no living accommodation, although some have been converted to dwellings. Such buildings, whose architectural features derive from local traditions of house building, provided space, light and access for workers. Whether such workers were employees or independent craftspeople hiring their accommodation, and whether spinning as well as weaving took place in the building, are questions which it is impossible to answer in the current state of knowledge. One of the most complex buildings in Saddleworth is High Kinders, the nucleus of

7 A block of cottages at New Delph, one of the townships of the parish of Saddleworth, a building constructed *c.* 1800. It incorporated four dwellings, each of two rooms and built two-on-two, with the upper dwellings approached from the high level at the rear, and two loomshops which ran across the second and third floors. When built, the dwellings were rented to four handloom-weavers. The block remained in single ownership but only in 1992 did it become a single dwelling. (Michael Stratton)

which is a farmstead of 1642 (8). Several ranges of buildings designed for textile manufactures were added, one of which has a taking-in door approached by a cantilevered staircase made of slabs of millstone grit.

Loomshops are numerous in Saddleworth, because handloom-weaving continued in the parish well into the second half of the nineteenth century, and because the millstone grit of which they are constructed is durable. Many loomshops, and buildings of similar dimensions accommodating spinning-jennies, were constructed in other textile regions but do not survive in significant numbers.

Saddleworth has buildings of even greater importance in understanding the evolution of

the factory from the workshop. The local poet Ammon Wrigley recalled in the early twentieth century:

> No more the carder makes his home
> Within the carding room;
> No more the weaver's porridge can
> Is hung against his loom.

His lines preserve a tradition that textile-workers made their homes among the machinery of the first generation of mills. Wrigley wrote of the 1840s:

> It was customary for the carder and his family to live in the mill, generally in one corner of the scribbling room, the living and sleeping apartment being divided from the machines by pieces of pack sheeting or canvas, sewn together and strung across the room from wall to wall. All the warmth in winter came from small fireplaces at each gable-end; even now some of our ruined old mills have little cottage chimneys on their roofs.

Shore Mill at Delph is rather smaller than some loomshop complexes in Saddleworth. It is

8 High Kinders, Saddleworth. The three- and four-storey buildings date from the mid-seventeenth century to the mid-nineteenth century. The taking-in door near the angle between the two main blocks is approached by a cantilevered stone staircase. The building in the foreground was once used as a dyehouse. The complex was once occupied by seven families engaged in the manufacture of textiles. (Barrie Trinder)

a three-storey, water-powered mill, with long-light windows on the top floor, built about 1780 (**colour plate 1**). In the corner is a small flue, precisely the little cottage chimney described by Wrigley. Brownhill Mill lies 2km (1 mile) to the south-west, and is also water-powered and of three storeys. It is a building of two distinct phases, which probably reflect its extension from a fulling mill to a carding and fulling mill in the late eighteenth century. As at Shore Mill, a cottage-style chimney protrudes from one corner of the roof (**9**). The census of 1841 shows that William Platt, a wool-carder, was living in the mill, with his wife and six children aged between 13 and 22 all engaged in slubbing or piecing woollen cloth, together with three younger children. Here certainly was a carder who, in Wrigley's words, 'makes his home/Within the carding room'.

Living among the machinery was commonplace in Saddleworth. In the 1850s a bride from Huddersfield marrying a Saddleworth man found her marriage bed was located between two looms in a room which also contained a fifty-spindle jenny, a bobbin wheel and a slubbing skip. The 'domestic system' involved not just the use of dwellings for manufacture, but also the use of purpose-built manufactories as habitations.

Stockings and silk

Other 'missing links' between the domestic workshop and the factory are provided by groups of dwellings designed to be used for manufacturing. At Calverton 11km (7 miles) north-east of Nottingham, birthplace of the stocking-frame in 1589, Windles Square consists of two (originally three) groups of cottages incorporating ground-floor workshops designed to accommodate stocking-frames. In the early nineteenth century fabrics as well as stockings came to be knitted in Nottinghamshire and Leicestershire necessitating the use of larger frames, which were accommodated in detached extensions to dwellings, of the type that house the museums of the knitting trade at Ruddington (**colour plate 2**) and Wigston.

Cash's Model Factory in Coventry encapsulates the last phases of domestic ribbon manufacture in that city. It consists of a terrace of two-storey cottages, with workshops above, where weavers were able to make use of a single source of power. The complex was built in 1857

9 Brownhill Mill, Saddleworth, an ancient fulling mill which appears to have been extended to incorporate carding machinery in the late eighteenth century. The 'cottage chimney' to the right is of the kind mentioned in Ammon Wrigley's poem. The 1841 census recorded that a wool-carder with his wife and children were sleeping in the mill. (Michael Stratton)

by John and Joseph Cash, but only 48 of 100 planned units were completed, and in 1862 the upper-storey workshops were converted to a single factory running over the tops of the dwellings.

Lighting

The Cottage Factory, Shore Mill and Brownhill Mill represent a significant development from such buildings as loomshops, in that their operation involved the generation, transmission and use of mechanical power, a topic considered in Chapter 2. There are other human needs which need to be met in a factory as much as in a home.

The characteristic Pennine loomshop windows demonstrate the importance of lighting in premises used for manufacturing, although dampness was a preferable option for weaving cotton and other fabrics, which were usually made in cellars. The first generation of factories could only repay the capital invested in them if they worked long hours, which necessitated the provision of artificial lighting. Visitors to Cromford in the 1780s were impressed that Richard Arkwright's mills worked throughout the night (colour plate 3). At that time millowners could only use candles or oil lamps for lighting workplaces. A favoured method was the Argand lamp, invented by the Frenchman Aimé Argand in 1782, which allowed a current of air to both the inner and outer surface of the flame, thus securing better combustion and a brighter light. It was estimated early in the nineteenth century that the equivalent of 452 candles were needed to illuminate the West Mill at Belper, and one factory master used to allow four candles to give light for each of his spinning-mules.

The illuminating properties of coal gas were demonstrated by William Murdock, who lit the counting-house at the Neath Abbey Ironworks in 1795–6. Murdock was employed by Boulton & Watt who from 1802 encouraged his experiments. The Salford Twist Mill was illuminated by a gas-lighting system designed by Murdock and supplied by Boulton & Watt in December 1805, shortly after a similar system had been installed in a factory in Halifax by one Samuel Clegg. Subsequently Boulton & Watt supplied gas-lighting equipment for other factories, but until mains supplies from public utility companies became available, in most towns from the 1820s, only the largest concerns used gas (10). A survey of 32 Gloucestershire mills in 1833 shows that 4 were lit entirely with candles, 6 with lamps, 18 with candles and lamps, 1 with lamps and gas, and 1 entirely with gas.

The value of maximizing natural lighting in manufacturing concerns is shown by the development of the north-lit shed. William Fairbairn in 1863 defined it as 'the shed principle lighted from the roof, or the "saw-tooth" principle ... chiefly adapted for power weaving'. Such sheds were being built in Manchester by the 1820s; one constructed in 1829 had a capacity for 600 power looms. A north-lit weaving shed was built as part of an integrated cottonworks – Orrell's Mill at Stockport – designed by Fairbairn in 1834–5. The north-lit shed was adopted in other textile regions, and in the late nineteenth century buildings of this type covered thousands of acres in the north Lancashire weaving region around Accrington and Burnley. It was also used in factories making consumer goods, such as footwear, clothing, food and furniture, and remained into the twentieth century one of the most common industrial building types. The same principle that underlay the north-lit shed – maximization of natural lighting – motivated the design of the daylight factory, developed in the United States in the early years of the twentieth century (see Chapter 8).

In more recent times the development of fluorescent lighting, and the need for a high degree of control of light, temperature and air purity, and for flexibility in the deployment of machines, as well as new constructional methods and materials, have led to the proliferation of windowless factories, clad in coated and corrugated steel.

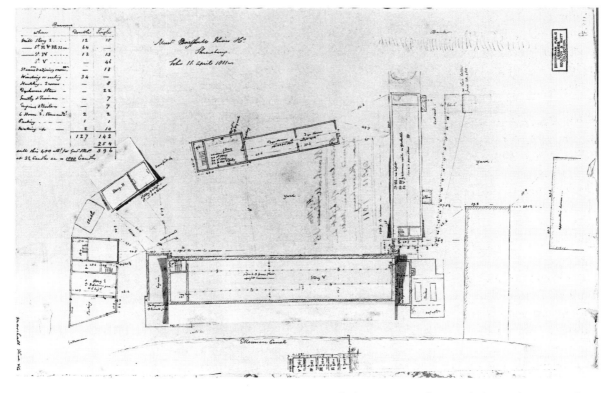

10 Some of the best plans of manufacturing complexes in the early nineteenth century are those drawn by employees of Boulton & Watt, prior to the installation of gas-lighting. The works of Marshall Hines & Co. shown on this plan is better known as the Ditherington Flax Mill, Shrewsbury, the first wholly iron-framed building, completed to the design of Charles Bage in 1797. The main mill is at the bottom of the plan. The other buildings from the left are the warehouse for outgoing products, the stable, the office and smiths' shop, the stove and dyehouse and the cross-wing or hackling block. The buildings shown in outline to the right are the flax warehouse and the apprentice house. The table in the top left corner shows the numbers of burners required in each part of the building. (Birmingham Reference Library)

Heating

Manufacturing concerns which employed furnaces, such as glassworks, ironworks and potbanks, did not need heating systems, but the efficient operation of textile mills, and subsequently of factories making consumer goods, depended on the dexterity of the workpeople, and fingers could only work well if workplaces were adequately heated. Many of the first generation of factories, such as Shore Mill at Saddleworth, were heated by simple, domestic-style open fires, which constituted a hazard where the atmosphere was laden with dust. William Strutt of Belper was a pioneer in the use of warm-air heating which appears to have been used in most of the early Derbyshire textile mills. The best surviving evidence of such a system is in part of Cromford Mill, Derbyshire; in Masson Mill, also at Cromford (**11**), and in the North Mill at Belper. In each mill there appears to have been a stove on the ground floor outside the main structure from which a flue ascended through the building, with outlets just below ceiling level on each floor, from which the circulation of hot air was aided by the draughts created by small fireplaces. The Salford Twist Mill, built by George Augustus Lee in 1800, was heated by steam which passed through the hollow cast-iron columns that formed the structure of the factory. The engineers Boulton & Watt supplied more than twenty similar systems for textile

11 Masson Mill, Cromford, Derbyshire, built by Richard Arkwright in 1784–5. The three bays with the Venetian and Diocletian windows projecting from the centre of the front elevation, beneath the cupola, accommodated staircases and lavatories. Inside the mill there remains evidence of its original heating system. Masson is a characteristic flagship mill (see Chapter 4) – the elegance of its buildings reflecting the wealth acquired by Richard Arkwright in the years since he had built the nearby Cromford Mill. (Barrie Trinder)

mills in the following two decades. They were employed only where boilers already existed for supplying steam engines. By the mid-nineteenth century hot-water systems provided a further option, but many factories continued to use open fires.

Washing

The deployment of large numbers of people in buildings concerned with manufacturing dictated the provision of sanitation systems. Privies appear to have been located on the main working-floors of the first generation of textile mills. Richard Arkwright's Masson Mill at Cromford, built in 1783–5, was probably the first in which privies were grouped around a staircase, housed, at Masson, in a projecting part of the front of the mill, beneath its Classical cupola (see **11**). In many subsequent mills privies were located within turrets which also housed staircases. Calver Mill in Derbyshire, a six-storey structure of *c.* 1805, has two octagonal towers which appear to have been built for this purpose. At Murray's Mill, Ancoats, Manchester, two parallel turrets can be observed, one contemporary with the building, the other, ornamented with external plumbing, apparently constructed when water-closets were installed. By 1900 enlightened companies were experimenting with special apparatus for their workpeople's washrooms, like the foot-operated handwasher for ceramics works preserved at the Coalport China Works Museum in Ironbridge, which obviated the need for potters with clay-encrusted hands to turn on taps. The fullest washing facilities were provided at coal mines. Pithead baths for miners leaving work were introduced in the 1880s in Germany where their provision became obligatory from 1900. In Britain it was not until the 1930s that pithead baths were constructed at most collieries.

Eating

It was and is necessary for factory managers to cater for other human needs normally met within the home, not least to allay hunger. Contrasting *laissez-faire* and paternalistic traditions can be observed from the earliest days of the Industrial Revolution. Most factory workers took food to their workplaces, and ate it amid the machines, just as the Saddleworth carders slept by their slubbing billies. In some areas traditions grew up that children took their fathers' food into their workplaces. Elsewhere junior employees would be sent out for fast food: pork pies, baked potatoes or, by 1900, fish-and-chips.

A few employers provided dining-rooms for their workpeople. In the dining-room at Saltaire Mill in the 1850s employees had the choice between a cheap meal prepared on the premises and food brought from home which could be warmed in communal ovens. There were dining-rooms at Bournville, Port Sunlight, and most of the model settlements (see Chapter 8) in Britain and overseas which were commended by the proponents of the ideal of the Garden City in the early twentieth century. At Bournville in 1905 there was accommodation for 2000 workers, who could obtain a roast meat dish with two vegetables for 4d. In the interests of increasing the output of munitions during World War I, the government urged manufacturers to follow the example of companies like Cadburys and Levers. It was argued that only by providing workers with a nutritious diet could their productivity be improved, and that the best means for doing this was by making food available at the workplace. Over a thousand works canteens had been established by 1918, which were used by more than a million workers (**12**). The policy of improving public health through communal feeding was carried further in World War II, through the provision of school meals and the establishment of 'British Restaurants' open to the public, but it was applied most vigorously in

12 The works canteen at the Daimler plant, the Motor Mills, Sandy Lane, Coventry, *c*. 1918. The canteen is located in a concrete-framed, multi-storey block of *c*. 1908. (Museum of British Road Transport, Coventry)

the workplace. All firms employing more than 250 workers were obliged to provide canteens, and smaller concerns were encouraged to do so. By December 1943 there were 10,577 works canteens in Britain, with a further 958 operating in ports and on building sites.

Most factory buildings are adapted by workers to meet their own needs. Certain areas, corners, spaces around windows, gaps between machines, the landings on blast furnaces, were and are marked out as the territories of individuals or groups, the tokens of possession being photographs of loved ones, football teams, political heroes, musicians or models. Such areas provide warmth, light for reading, and space for momentary relaxation and consumption of food and drink.

Sociability

During the 1920s and 1930s some companies in 'new' industries, such as food manufacturing and the production of household appliances, were anxious that their premises should help to convey favourable images to the public. Pictures of factories appeared in advertisements and on packaging. Such companies also sought reputations as good employers, and provided well-publicized washrooms, dining-halls, health centres, training facilities, social clubs and playing fields for their employees. These were features of a particular stage of social development, when most employees at a factory were drawn from surrounding communities, when domestic entertainment was confined to the radio, and when most people travelled by public transport. The mobility provided by the motor car, and changes in patterns of popular culture and social aspirations, have led to the decline of such facilities. At the Welgar Shredded Wheat factory in Welwyn Garden City, buildings now cover the football pitch and much of the space used for welfare facilities has been put to other uses. An illustration of the past importance of social provision is provided at the Stanton Gate pipeworks north of Nottingham where the production buildings – huge sheds with steel

frames clad with sheeting – have been demolished, while the welfare facilities – the exhibition hall, the training centre and the sports club, brick buildings of some style – still line the sparsely used concrete roads of what was once a vast manufacturing complex.

Stairs, hoists and lifts

In every building used in manufacturing it is necessary to provide access for raw materials and for the removal of finished products. The vertical shaft in the traditional English water corn mill has a power take-off on an upper floor, driving a hoist by which sacks of grain are raised from the ground to a taking-in door on the bin floor. Hand-operated hoists were installed in most multi-storey malthouses, enabling sacks of barley to be raised to taking-in doors adjacent to the steeping tanks on each floor. In premises used for manufacturing textiles, whether loomshops or large factories, the presence or absence of taking-in doors may indicate the kinds of materials and products for which the buildings were designed. Loomshops where bulky pieces of woollen cloth were woven have such doors, but in some large factory buildings, such as Ditherington Flax Mill in Shrewsbury, materials were handled in quantities which could be carried on the staircases. By the 1830s elevators, called teagles, were in use in some Lancashire cotton mills and warehouses. They had cages or platforms guided by vertical rails, which linked the floors of the buildings concerned, power being provided by the mill's line-shafting. In 1848 Jesse Hartley, engineer of the Liverpool Docks, ordered a pair of hydraulic lifts from (Sir) William Armstrong for use in warehouses. The passenger lift was subsequently developed in the United States by Elisha Graves Otis, who demonstrated his fail-safe technology for elevators in 1854. In due course such technology was applied to elevators whose motive power was derived from electric motors.

By 1900 the means of conveying materials in factories were becoming more sophisticated. Belt conveyors were used for horizontal

13 The western elevation of malting No. 7 at Mistley, Essex, built by Free, Rodwell & Co. in 1904. This was the largest building in one of the largest malting complexes in England, and exemplified the most advanced techniques of the time, not just in the process of malting, but in the bulk handling of barley and malt by means of bucket elevators, augers and belts. (Barrie Trinder)

transport of substances like grain or coal, which were sometimes moved upwards by augers. Pneumatic systems enabled some materials to be carried around factories in large pipes. The complex means of conveying barley in the large maltings constructed around the turn of the century, such as those at Mistley, Essex (**13**), represent a substantial advance on the simple hoists of earlier malthouses. Modern systems of lifts and conveyors provide precisely the same access, for people and materials, as the cantilevered staircase which runs up to the taking-in door at High Kinders at Saddleworth.

Asserting authority

A new feature of the Industrial Revolution period was the architectural expression of social discipline. New means of organizing production and the investment of large sums of money in buildings and machinery led factory owners to demand punctual and regular attendance. The cupolas and clocks which adorn many factory buildings were a means of enforcing that discipline.

The immediate surroundings of a factory could also express social hegemony, marking off territory where power was held by the entrepreneur. A factory was a clearly defined area, cut off from the outside world. Cromford Mill is a significant archetype. It occupies a distinct territory, bounded by high rocks which separate it from the River Derwent, its later buildings acting as a wall protecting the complex from the road which leads to Lea. The principle that a factory was an area cut off from the outside world was recognized in a description of the largest fustian works in Warrington in 1863, of which, it was said, 'on the principle of the factory, [this] works is the only one with all the premises shut off within gates'. A factory wall was not just an insurance against theft and the intrusions of Luddites. It

14 Asserting hegemony – the boundary of the Hunslet Mill flax-spinning complex in Leeds is marked not just by the imposing presence of a seven-storey spinning mill of 1838–40, but by an extensive wall which surrounds the whole site (see also **24**). (RCHME)

was also an assertion of the rights of property. By demarcating his factory the owner proclaimed his control over the production process (**14**).

Accommodating people

The archaeological evidence provided by historic industrial buildings can be viewed in several contexts: as architecture, as one development in the history of construction, or as an indication of how production has been organized at different periods. It can also be seen as a reflection of how accommodation has been organized to cater for human needs, for working-space, for power, for heating, lighting and sanitation, and for access. Seeing the factory in these terms reveals a degree of continuity which is lacking when it is interpreted purely as architecture or as the application of constructional techniques. In this context there is no essential break between domestic and factory production. A distinctly different stage is reached when power is applied to manufacturing processes, but it was still necessary to meet human needs. Only a few people, like the carders of Saddleworth, actually slept in factory buildings, but many did and still do spend in them large parts of their lives.

2
Accommodating power

The use of power in production processes has sometimes been seen as one of the essential characteristics of a factory. Andrew Ure wrote in 1835 that the factory system consisted of 'the combined operation of many orders of workpeople ... tending with assiduous skill a system of productive machines continuously impelled by a central power'. Some early factories lacked power. Their purpose might be to concentrate several forms of hand production, or to create a disciplined working environment. Nevertheless the application of power was one of the features which marked the evolution of the factory during the Industrial Revolution.

The characteristic prime movers of that period were waterwheels and steam engines. Water-power was used to operate one textile manufacturing process, the fulling of woollen cloth, from the late Middle Ages, and had provided power for metalworking from the sixteenth century. In the course of the eighteenth century it was used to throw silk, and to spin cotton, wool and flax, as well as to work carding machines and looms. Engineers in the late eighteenth century devoted much energy to increasing the efficiency of water-power. The steam engine was first set to practical use about 1712, when an engine designed by Thomas Newcomen began to pump water from a coal mine near Dudley. About 100 such engines were employed for pumping, chiefly from mines, by 1733, but they could be used in generating

rotative power for machines only by using them to recirculate water from a pool below a waterwheel to a reservoir situated above it. The first system of this kind appears to have been that used to work the bellows and hammers of the Coalbrookdale ironworks in the early 1740s. The efficiency of the steam engine was improved by James Watt, whose first working engines began to operate in 1776. In 1782 Watt perfected a rotative engine that could work machinery directly, by which time others, by using cranks, were obtaining rotative motion from Newcomen engines. The first use of rotative steam power in a cotton mill appears to have been at Papplewick Mill, Nottinghamshire, in 1786.

By 1800 well over 2000 steam engines were in use in Britain, fulfilling many functions in mines, ironworks and textile mills, pumping water for drinking and for filling canals, grinding grain in flour mills, and serving various purposes in oil mills, potteries, chemical works and paper mills. Nevertheless steam-power was of less consequence in manufacturing than water-power, and remained so until the 1820s, although by 1870 it has been estimated that steam supplied 93.6 per cent of the needs of British industry compared with 6.4 per cent supplied by water-power, which is a measure of the growth of manufacturing in the nineteenth century rather than of the abandonment of water-power, since the power output of many mills was increased from the 1850s by the application of turbines.

15 Rowley's Mansion, Shrewsbury, the first significant brick building in the town, constructed in 1618–19 as an extension of the great timber house erected by William Rowley about twenty years earlier. In the early nineteenth century the mansion was used as a flannel factory, power being derived from a gin operated by a chestnut mare. (Barrie Trinder)

Horses or donkeys, trotting on circular tracks, were also significant sources of power in the Industrial Revolution. They pumped water or raised minerals from many mines. In breweries horses operated water pumps, and in textiles powered many spinning-jenny and spinning-mule shops between the 1780s and the 1820s. A flannel manufactory in Shrewsbury in the early nineteenth century, located in the seventeenth-century Rowley's Mansion, had carding machines and jennies operated by a single chestnut mare (**15**).

Many factories of the Industrial Revolution period used more than one source of power. Stanley Mill, Gloucestershire, was built in 1813 as a water-powered woollen cloth mill, its five waterwheels producing about 200hp. A steam

engine was installed in 1814, but its output was only 40hp, and it could only ever have been a supplement to the waterwheels. The most diverse sources of power were those at Sutton Mill near Mansfield, rebuilt by Samuel Unwin from an earlier building some time before 1784, which drew power from a waterwheel, a steam engine and from a windmill.

Transmitting power

The transmission of power was one of the key innovations of the factories of the Industrial Revolution. In earlier applications of mechanical power the source of power was essentially a part of the machine. In a water corn mill, the waterwheel transmitting power to millstones and hoists through a pitwheel, a wallower and a vertical shaft, can be seen as just one component of a single machine.

The builders of the first mechanized factories in the eighteenth century subdivided the power derived from a single source of energy, usually a waterwheel or a steam engine, to power many machines in such structures as textile mills, machine shops in engineering works and lead-dressing plants. Power was transmitted from prime mover to productive machine by line shafts and belts. In the first mechanized textile factories in Britain, the silk mills of the Midlands of which John Lombe's mill at Derby of 1721 was the first (see 6), and the thirty-bay, five-storey Old Mill at Congleton of 1753 the largest (16), power was transmitted from waterwheels along horizontal shafts linked by toothed gearing to vertical shafts, which drove the large circular throwing machines extending through the ground and first floors, and the ranks of small winding machines on the floors above. In Richard Arkwright's first water-powered cotton-spinning factory, erected at Cromford in 1771, power was conveyed to carding machines and to the water frames which were used for spinning by means of wooden drums and leather belts. The system is well illustrated by the eighteenth-century water frame exhibited at the Helmshore Textile Museum, Lancashire. The principles which lay behind British systems of power transmission were formalized in the 1820s by William Fairbairn and James Lillie. It was Fairbairn, when renewing the transmission system at Murray's Mill, Manchester in 1817, who began to substitute shafts of turned wrought iron for the heavier cast-iron shafts used previously.

16 A reconstruction drawing of the possible original arrangement of machinery in the Old Mill, Congleton. Eleven circular silk-throwing machines were housed on the ground floor, with winding machines above. (RCHME)

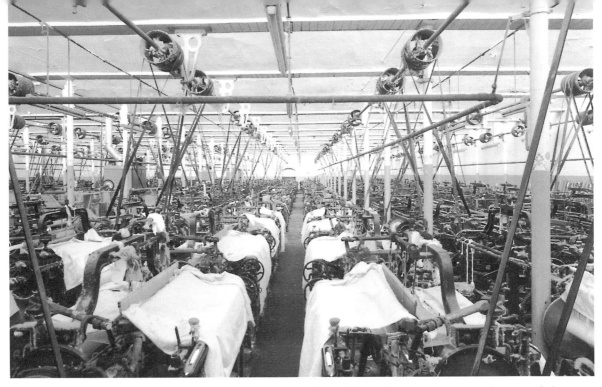

17 The single-storey north-lit weaving shed at Queen Street Mill, Harle Syke, Burnley, built in 1894, where power is supplied by a tandem compound steam engine by Robert of Nelson, via a conventional system of line shafts and belts. There are now over 300 Lancashire looms in the shed, but there were over 1000 in the early years of the twentieth century. (Michael Stratton)

These patterns were followed in innumerable factories. Power was conveyed from prime movers through horizontal shafts and toothed gearing to vertical shafts, which, through further toothed gearing, drove horizontal shafts on each floor of the building, from which individual machines were driven by leather belts and pulleys (**17**). Horizontal line shafts were usually between 2m (6½ft) and 5m (16½ft) in length, were coupled together so that they could extend along the full length of a mill floor (which might be over 60m/197ft), and carried on bearings mounted on hangers or brackets, which might be attached to the outer walls or to bolting faces – the flattened top sections of the cylindrical columns which supported the internal structure of the mill. Columns with bolting faces were used in the 1820s at Beehive Mill, Manchester, and in Mill D in Marshall's Mill, Leeds, but

they did not become commonplace until the 1850s (**18**). In some factories it is possible to observe blocked cast-iron portals through which shafting entered working-floors, while walls may be lined by the stubs of redundant brackets. Plugged holes in ceilings may indicate where short vertical shafts conveyed power from horizontal shafts to machines on the floors above. The course of shafting is also indicated by oil stains, since every bearing and journal required constant lubrication. A 60m (197ft) long, five-storey textile mill in the 1830s might have 450m (1476ft) of iron shafting, which, with its attendant couplings, pulleys and hangers, might weigh as much as 20 tons, and require a prime mover producing between 50 and 70hp to work it. Saltaire Mill, completed in 1853, is 167m (548ft) long and had 3000m (9843ft) of shafting, weighing over 60 tons, necessitating engines with an output of 1250hp to operate the machinery.

Toothed gearing, line-shafting and leather belts remained the principal means of transmitting power in British factories throughout the nineteenth century (**colour plate 4**). The rope-drive system, in which power was conveyed from grooved pulleys on the flywheels of a steam engine, to shafting on each floor of a building by means of ropes, was introduced in Belfast in the 1850s, and was the standard means of transmission in Lancashire cotton mills in the last quarter of the nineteenth century. The system can be observed at Trencherfield Mill (**colour plate 5**), which forms part of the Wigan Pier complex. Rope drive was used in other industries, in brickworks and iron-rolling mills for example, but line-shafting remained in use in many British manufacturing plants in the mid-twentieth century. In the 1930s the machine shop at the Lagonda motor-car works at Staines still used line-shafting, the torque from which threatened to destroy the ramshackle sheds at the start of each working day.

18 The transmission of power from the steam engine to the looms at Upper Tean Mill, Staffordshire, an iron-framed building of 1823. The upright, cylindrical cast-iron columns have been designed and cast with flattened edges to accommodate shafting, and it appears that at this point vertical shafts connected with horizontal shafts, the former descending through a space at the point where the parts of the iron cross-members abut, and through a hole in the masonry. Doubtless this reflects several phases of transmission. The horizontal pipes are part of a later heating system. (Michael Stratton)

Hydraulic and electric power

Factories were gradually transformed by the application of a principle, recognized early in the nineteenth century, for which an appropriate technology developed only slowly – that of inserting a converter of energy alongside the prime mover, installing a more efficient mode of transmission, and powering machines by individual secondary motors. Several attempts were made to do this in the mid-nineteenth century. Hydraulic transmission, developed by Sir William Armstrong, was applied in seaports to work-cranes, hoists, lock-gates and lifting bridges, and in the textile warehouses of Manchester and Nottingham to power presses and lifts, but not in most forms of manufacturing industry. Systems for supplying steam to small engines working individual machines proved thermally inefficient. Compressed-air systems, developed in the 1860s during the excavation of the Hoosac tunnel, Massachusetts, and the Mont Cenis tunnel beneath the Alps, proved important as a means of powering drills in mines, and in certain specialized applications in factories.

The principle of transmitting power from a central source was articulated to the Royal Society of Arts in 1893 by W. C. Unwin, who declared, 'Energy ... is to be considered as a commodity which can be manufactured in a convenient form, distributed and sold.' Unwin's arguments led towards 'central' power stations, the first of which, in Pearl Street, New York, was opened in 1882 by Thomas Edison. The first textile mills to use electric power generated electricity on site, usually with generators driven by steam turbines in separate power houses. From these, cables led to electric motors on each floor, located for reasons of fire safety in rectangular turrets, which drove conventional shafting systems, a system known as 'group drive' (**19**). The first mill to use electric power in the Manchester region was Falcon Mill, Bolton, built between 1904 and 1908. It was not long before electricity from the mains was used to power similar systems, one of the first installations to do this being part of Murray's Mill in Ancoats, Manchester, which was

rebuilt in 1908. Steam engines used to generate electricity can be seen in the power hall of the Museum of Science and Industry in Manchester. As the twentieth century progressed, smaller electric motors were applied to power individual machines in textile mills, and indeed in all types of manufacturing concern. The store adjacent to the fitters' workshop, with reserve supplies of electric motors ranged on shelves for instant installation in the case of breakdown, is as characteristic of twentieth-century factories as line-shafting was of those of the nineteenth century.

19 Kearsley Mill, Bolton, completed in 1906, an apparently typical Lancashire cotton-spinning mill of the early twentieth century. Cotton was spun by mules, with a total of 117,999 spindles. Power was provided not by typical Lancashire mill engines but by steam turbo-generators, providing current for electric motors working line-shafting on each floor, housed in the projecting tower, and for three motors operating the preparation machinery on the ground floor. Kearsley Mill has concrete floors supported by steel beams and cast-iron columns. (Michael Stratton)

3
The changing complex

A factory is usually not a single building but a group of structures clustered round a courtyard, with its outer perimeter ringed by a wall defining the area over which the entrepreneur enjoys hegemony. High land costs, the need to distribute power and heat, and to minimize the time and effort expended in carrying materials from one process to the next, dictated that most textile mills, like those considered in the last two chapters, were relatively compact groups of buildings. One of the largest was Murray's Mills, Ancoats, Manchester, which evolved from 1798 into a vast complex of eight production blocks and warehouses. After the publication in 1831 of an engraving of the mill, it became one of the stock images of the Industrial Revolution (20, 21).

With other technologies a more sprawling layout was appropriate. Even in textile manufactures, potentially noxious processes like dyeing, bleaching or calico printing would often be confined to a peripheral part of a mill complex, or even to a separate works, but the strongest contrast is provided by explosives factories. The risks of conflagration during the manufacture of gunpowder led, before the end of the eighteenth century, to the construction of single-storey buildings set well apart and with a high perimeter fence or wall to provide security. The Royal Gunpowder Factory at Waltham Abbey, Essex, which developed over 300 years, provides the best example (22). Originally a fulling mill was adapted to blend gunpowder. As production expanded, water from the River Lea was employed to power small waterwheels and to transport materials across the site. New buildings were constructed in the mid-nineteenth century – long terraces of workshops with substantial outer walls and lightweight roofs, designed to ensure that the force of any explosion would be directed upwards (23). Power was conveyed by underground shafting from steam engines in the centre of each terrace to the blending pans in each workshop. Gunpowder production proceeded from south to north across the site, ending at the Grand Magazine. When Waltham Abbey turned to the manufacture of the more unstable high explosives, like guncotton, the same workshops were used, although the steam engines and the underground shafting were no longer required, and the orientation of production was changed, with the materials moving southwards across the site.

Many manufacturing processes were originally undertaken in the open rather than within buildings. The production in cities of intricate machines like firearms utilized streets as production lines, as the products of craftsmen working in individual workshops to produce locks, barrels or stocks were brought together in other workshops to be assembled into guns. Many individual factories developed in the same way, with materials being carried between workshops across courtyards, in which the central open space might be used for noisy or noxious processes. Further courtyards might

20 Cotton factories, Union Street, Manchester, a steel engraving by McGahey after J. Harwood, which appears in George Pyne, *Lancashire Illustrated ... from original drawings*, published by Nicholson & Co. in 1831. The engraving shows the factories alongside the Rochdale Canal in Ancoats. In the centre stand Murray's Old Mill of 1798 and Decker Mill of 1802. In the background is Old Mill constructed by McConnel & Kennedy in 1798, and Sedgwick Mill, built in 1818–20. (Ironbridge Gorge Museum Trust)

21 Ground plan of Murray's Mills, Manchester, showing: A: Old Mill, 1798, B: Decker Mill, 1802, C: New Mill, 1804, D: Murray Street block, *c.* 1804–6, E: Bengal Street block, *c.* 1804–6, F: canal basin, G: mid-nineteenth-century engine house, H: partly rebuilt engine house of New Mill, I: Doubling Mill, 1842, J: Fireproof Mill, *c.* 1842, K: New Little Mill, 1908, L: site of former engine house, 1802. (RCHME)

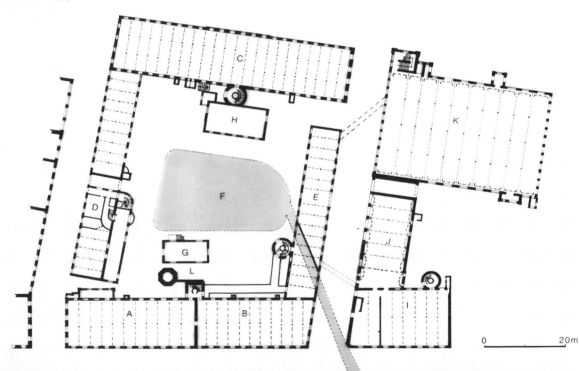

22 An aerial view from the south of the Waltham Abbey
Gunpowder works, Essex, alongside the River Lea. The
dispersed nature of the site can readily be appreciated.
Some of the buildings are linked by a canal system which
runs through the centre of the site. (RCHME)

23 A mid-nineteenth-century building at Waltham Abbey,
designed for the manufacture of gunpowder. A steam
engine, in the central section, powered blending machines
in the six bays ranged on either side, through underfloor
shafting. The stout walls and lightweight roofs were
designed to ensure that the force of any explosion went
upwards rather than outwards. In the early twentieth
century the same workshops were adapted for the
manufacture of high explosives. The windows along the
frontage were installed after World War II when the works
became a research establishment. (Barrie Trinder)

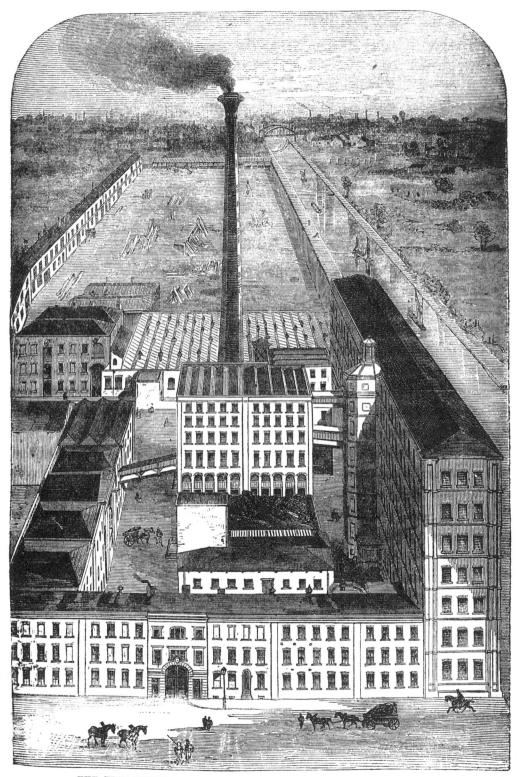

THE FLAX-SPINNING MILLS OF MESSRS. WILKINSON AND CO., LEEDS.

24 The courtyard layout of Hunslet Mill, Leeds, is evident in this view from George Measom's *Guide to the Great Northern Railway*, published *c.* 1860. The three-storey warehouse and office range fronting Goodman Street in the foreground was rebuilt in the 1840s. The seven-storey range alongside the River Aire was constructed in 1838–40. The turret containing privies and a staircase can be seen on the courtyard side. In the centre of the complex is the steam engine and boiler house, behind which is a range of north-lit sheds, and the drying grounds (see also **14**). (Ironbridge Gorge Museum Trust)

develop as new processes or products were introduced creating complex sites in which the Victorians took great pride (**24**). Subsequently, progressive ideals of industrial management, largely developed in the United States, encouraged the simpler layouts of the 'model factories', considered in Chapter 8.

Farmyards and courtyards

Early factories shared many features with farmyards. In both, courtyards provided security while ensuring adequate space, lighting and fresh air. Research at the Upper Forge in Coalbrookdale has shown that an ironworking building constructed in the mid-eighteenth century had open sides, just like a farm building. Boundary walls in factories prevented the theft of goods rather than the straying of livestock. In both factories and farmyards, the introduction of prime movers, whether waterwheels, horse gins or steam engines, encouraged a differentiation between processes that needed power and those that depended solely on human energy. The prevalence of courtyard layouts and the focal importance of powered machinery is apparent in the layout of such farm museums as Acton Scott, Shropshire.

A steam engine and its attendant boiler house would often form the node of a factory. Large works had several engines and hence several nodes. Machinery would be located in the same or an adjoining building to minimize the power loss through bearings and gears. A structure that accommodated expensive machinery would

inevitably be among the best-built at the factory, and might provide support for lean-to workshops. Elsewhere the node might not be a steam engine but a durable structure housing a heating process. One or more blast furnaces might be the focus of an ironworks – as can be seen with the surviving examples at Ironbridge: Coalbrookdale, Bedlam and Blists Hill. An English glass cone might be the initial focus of a glassworks as at the Redhouse Works, Stourbridge, West Midlands (**25**, **26**). Electric power was an important agent in liberating factory planning, once each machine was driven by its integral motor rather than from a central power source. In many fields of production, the powered final assembly line has become the focus of the works, its appetite for components being fed by ancillary workshops and stores.

A basic format, for both farms and early factories, of sheds arranged round one or more courtyards, allowed for adaptation and growth. New technologies could be adopted without having to cease work, demolish and rebuild anew. In examining industrial complexes a contrast can be observed between a rural tradition – drawn from farms, mines and brickyards – and a more constrained and architecturally self-conscious urban world of, for example, potteries and brassworks. The two

25 A postcard showing the accumulation of factory buildings around glass cones at Wordsley near Stourbridge, *c.* 1900. (Collection of Dr Paul Collins)

26 A glass cone, all that remains of a glassworks complex at Lemington, west of Newcastle upon Tyne. (Barrie Trinder)

are not exclusive. An estate farm could have the formality of an urban factory, while a city gasworks might consist of a gaggle of assorted structures all lacking any aesthetic quality.

Mines and smelters

A mine is not normally regarded as a factory, but a study of coal and metal-ore mines highlights the rambling unconstrained nature of most industrial complexes in rural areas. The focus of a mine, around which other structures and activities were arranged, was the shaft, with its headstock and winder. Early mines often took the form of shallow bell pits, which were abandoned, as the roof started to fall, for further pits nearby. Shafts became more permanent as they became deeper. From the 1790s steam engines came to be used for winding coal and men, as well as for pumping out water.

The precise layout of a nineteenth- or twentieth-century coal mine depended on the size of the operation and on whether men and coal were lifted out of the same or separate shafts. The buildings of Caphouse Colliery, West Yorkshire, the only coal mine in England where visitors can go underground, are clustered around the timber headgear and the engine house of 1876 with its horizontal winder, although access to the workings can also be gained through an adit.

In the late nineteenth century the variety of surface buildings at large coal mines increased with advances in mining technology and growing concern for safety (**27**). Many mines were equipped with steam-driven fans to aid ventilation. Air compressors, again often steam-powered, were installed to operate drills and other equipment. The introduction of safety lamps led to the construction of lamp rooms. Screens with mechanical jiggers were built to separate coal into grades of different sizes, and washers were installed to remove dust. Power stations were built to provide electricity. In the twentieth century, and especially in the 1930s, pithead baths were constructed, many in a modernist style inspired by the Dutch architect W. M. Dudok. All these structures would be clustered as closely as possible around the shafts used for transporting men and coal.

The only pre-nationalization coal-mining complexes in England which are in any way complete are Caphouse and the much larger Chatterley Whitfield mine in Staffordshire, which once employed over 4000 men, but many components of former mines are conserved as monuments or have been adapted to new uses. Early forms of winding technology are represented by horse-gin circles at Jane Pit, Workington, Saltom Colliery, Whitehaven, and Ram Hill Pit, Westerleigh, near Bristol. There are steam winding engines at Elsecar in South Yorkshire and at F Pit, Washington, Co. Durham. Numerous engine houses survive without their engines, among the more notable being those at Bestwood, Nottinghamshire, and Friars Goose at Gateshead Fell in Co. Durham. A winding house which accommodated electrically powered machinery remains at Ledstone Luck Colliery in West Yorkshire, and a colliery power station building with adjacent streets called Voltage Terrace and Electric Crescent, at Philadelphia in Co. Durham.

Coal-using manufactures were often situated in close proximity to mines (**28**). Brickmaking and limeburning were often among the principal business activities of the owners of small rural mines, and brickworks and limekilns were located near to mine shafts. At Vobster Breach mine in Somerset are remains of two ranks of

front-loading coke ovens built in the 1860s. In the twentieth century several power stations for public supply have been erected alongside the coal mines which supplied their fuel, notable examples being at Agecroft, Manchester, and Rugeley in Staffordshire.

Mines worked for ores of such non-ferrous metals as lead, tin and copper share many of the same components as coal mines. Magpie lead mine in Derbyshire is a well-preserved example where there is a headstock, an engine house, a boiler house, two winding houses and a power house. Most non-ferrous mines in England closed before 1900, and facilities for the workers were basic compared with those of twentieth-century collieries. The most impressive leadworking complexes are found in the Yorkshire Dales and Co. Durham, where, during the eighteenth and nineteenth centuries, mines were closely associated with smelters. Furnaces and stores might, as at Grassington, be enclosed within perimeter walls. One of the most distinctive buildings associated with a lead

27 The coal mine at Creswell, near Worksop, Derbyshire, showing the sprawl of buildings around the two headstocks. The colliery was built by the Bolsover Colliery Co. between 1894 and 1897. The two shafts were both 18ft (5.5m) in diameter, and originally extended down 445yd (407m) to the Top Hard seam. (RCHME)

28 Aerial view of the coke and by-products plant at Orgreave, Yorkshire, showing links with adjacent collieries and railways. (Ironbridge Gorge Museum Trust)

smelter is the open-sided peat store at Old Gang in Swaledale, which extends for 120m (394ft) along the valley side (**29**). Essential components of lead smelters where reverberatory furnaces were employed, were lengthy flues, carrying away noxious gases and terminating in chimneys high on the adjacent hillsides. The most spectacular examples are at Allendale in Northumberland (**colour plate 6**).

Rural and suburban brickworks

Ceramics works, especially those making bricks and roofing-tiles, have much in common with mines in their layout and in their continuity of basic form from the early years of the Industrial Revolution. Brick clay, a raw material of low value, was logically worked close to where it was dug. Brickworks typically have a sprawling layout, the central processing plant being surrounded by kilns, most of the land area being taken up by claypits and level ground for stockpiling burnt bricks.

The simplest brickworks were factories without any buildings. The 'stock' bricks of London were made by the same means for over 200 years after the Great Fire of 1666. Clay was dug on open land, left to weather over a winter and then tempered in the open air before being pressed on a moulding stool. The bricks were simply piled up in hacks for drying, and then in clamps for burning. The same site might be used from one season to the next, but as London expanded, from around 1800, so new sites on the fringe of the city were opened up. Even the introduction of machinery in the form of horse-driven pugmills, did not necessitate buildings. Permanent structures in the form of circular or rectangular kilns were first provided at estate yards that evolved into commercial works in the late eighteenth century. A sand house and drying shed would be provided in addition to a rectangular kiln. The erection of crude hovels for the moulders permitted production to continue throughout the year. The brick and pottery works that were established on the outskirts of London were often worked for a few years until the clay was exhausted, after which the land was covered with houses.

The development in the 1830s and 1840s of more sophisticated machinery, for clay preparation and for pressing and extruding bricks, justified the construction of factory buildings, together with steam engines and their associated boilers. The Hathern Station Brick and Terracotta Works located to the north of Loughborough was established in 1874 to exploit a claybank behind the factory and to allow goods, initially facing-bricks, to be dispatched across Britain by the Midland Railway (30). Pugmills, grinding pans and

29 View of Old Gang Lead Smelting works, North Yorkshire. The peat store is located to the left, further up the hillside. (Michael Stratton)

extrusion machines were located in sheds arranged around the steam engine. Circular and rectangular kilns which had no need for power were set away from the central block. As the works expanded, new workshops were erected for hand-pressed wares and to house engineering workshops and offices. Ancillary buildings were basic in form, and constructed of waste bricks, terracotta and faience.

The same principles in terms of industrial layout apply to the huge brickworks built in the Midlands to exploit the shale-like clay discovered at Fletton near Peterborough in 1881. The Lower Oxford clay contains enough organic combustible material to reduce fuel consumption in the kiln by about two-thirds. Several large plants were established from the 1890s. The most impressive was located south of Bedford. By the 1930s it was acknowledged to be 'the largest brickworks in the world' and took its name, Stewartby, from the chairman of

30 The Hathern Brick and Terracotta works, alongside the main line of the Midland Railway, north of Loughborough, Leicestershire. The clay-preparation section can be seen in the middle of the works. Both circular and rectangular kilns are arranged around the perimeter of the works with the original claypit to the right, and a dumping ground for old moulds and rejected wares in the background. (Ironbridge Gorge Museum Trust)

the London Brick Company & Forders Ltd (**31**). Workers were housed in a model village with extensive communal facilities. Mechanical navvies fed clay via inclines and light railways to roller crushers and rows of presses housed in the central production building. The bricks were then transferred to one of the huge Hoffman kilns – rectangular structures with oval firing chambers, in which the fire travelled round in a loop with a fresh batch of bricks being set and withdrawn for each circuit.

Urban potteries

The potteries of the six towns of north Staffordshire also have rural roots, although they were engulfed by canals, railways and terraced houses. In the seventeenth century a potworks might be developed from a farmstead.

Clay was mixed and ware dried in the open. A barn might be used for storage and a kiln erected on the end of the farmhouse or in the farmyard. As the scale of production developed so purpose-built drying-houses were provided along with secure warehouses.

Several purpose-built works were erected around Fenton and Burslem in the middle years of the eighteenth century, complete with throwing-houses and warehouses, and usually with an impressive street frontage. The courtyard format became more tightly defined and the density of building in the towns increased. The small courtyards and exterior staircases characteristic of north Staffordshire potbanks were adopted, reputedly to segregate workers as a way of enforcing discipline, and to preserve the secrets of those involved in glazing and decorating. Larger works would have workshops for grinding raw materials and for making the saggars, the clay tubs that protected delicate tableware when it was in the kiln. Some early nineteenth-century potbanks were laid out around large courtyards, like that at the Gladstone Pottery Museum, Longton. Production progressed from the rear of the premises, where a steam engine drove clay-preparation machinery,

31 The Stewartby brickworks of the London Brick Company, photographed from the air in 1959. In the background are the claypits and the railway sidings, which were used both to bring in coal and to dispatch bricks. Several of the highly distinctive Hoffman kilns can be seen to the right. In the left foreground is part of the model village of Stewartby, built by the LBC in the early 1930s. (London Brick Co.)

forward to the slip house, kilns, and dippers' house where glazes were applied. The rooms at the front were used for final decorating, storage, display and dispatch.

Most potbanks showed a polite face to the outside world, a formal street frontage of two or three storeys masking a congested and frequently changing world of workshops and bottle ovens. A frontage building was of regular if not symmetrical appearance. It ranged on either side of a central wagon arch, beneath a Venetian window, above which was a pediment. Within the pediment the date or name of the building might be inscribed on an elliptical lozenge. Some potbanks had cupolas behind their pediments. The typical or idiomatic frontage building (see Chapter 4) took inspiration from the formal façade of Josiah Wedgwood's Etruria, which itself faced a canal not a road. This pottery, built between 1767 and 1773 to the designs of the architect Joseph Pickford of Derby, comprised three blocks of buildings, each with hovels containing kilns at each corner.

The traditional frontage could be adapted to a corner site, as at Enoch Wood's Fountain Place works, at Burslem, of 1789. The

Middleport Pottery of Burgess and Leigh, built in 1888, is more utilitarian in expression, with a plain brick pediment set above an asymmetrically placed entrance. The works, which remains in operation with its fabric largely unaltered, was a late Victorian attempt to update the layout of the Staffordshire potbanks. Wares were transferred across the site from one parallel range to the next, with the firing kilns conveniently located between the 'green house' and the dippers' hot house, and a row of glazing kilns set between the hot house and the warehouse block.

Charles Lynam, a Staffordshire architect, developed a linear arrangement for the Minton Hollins decorative tile factory, developed from 1867 in the centre of Stoke-on-Trent. The raw materials were forwarded from the slip houses at the back of the site to the tilemaking workshops, the decorating shops and oven being

set next in line. The warehouses and packing house were grouped into a formal two-storey frontage, the façade being set with geometric tiles. Lynam designed two further tileworks at Jackfield, just downstream from the Iron Bridge in Shropshire. Both Craven Dunnill, built in 1871–4 and now the Jackfield Tile Museum, and Maws, dating from 1883 and now a craft centre, were given long, linear plans (32, 33). These more expansive layouts, hybrids between an urban pottery and a rural brickworks, reflect the semi-rural setting, and the need to fit the works within a narrow valley, parallel to the river and the railway.

A courtyard layout surrounded by two-storey workshops was used for potteries in other parts of England, including Brannam's in the centre of Barnstaple, north Devon, which was established around 1840 and given a new arched entrance façade in 1886–9 (see 46). The significance of this type of layout thus extends beyond the Staffordshire Potteries and indeed beyond the ceramics industry. It is characteristic of most urban manufactures where precision work by hand was combined with the use of power. It is to be found in factories making clocks or glass, and in many engineering works.

West Midlands workshops

The domestic origins of the courtyard layout and its versatility can be seen most clearly in the

32 The tileworks of Maw & Co. at Jackfield in the Ironbridge Gorge, designed by Charles Lynam, and opened in 1883. The longitudinal arrangement of the works is evident from this touched-up late Victorian photograph. Raw materials are delivered, some of them by rail, at the eastern end of the works to the right; clay preparation powered by a steam engine takes place in the central portion of the site, beyond which are the kilns and beyond them the offices and showrooms. (Ironbridge Gorge Museum Trust)

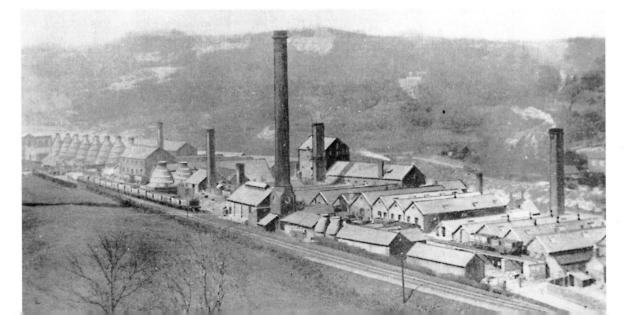

33 The ornate entrance to the works of Maw & Co. at Jackfield, in which the company's own tiles are used to proclaim the purpose of the building. The company was established in Worcester in 1850, moved to Benthall in the Ironbridge Gorge in 1852, and then to the nearby Jackfield site in 1883. Above and around the entrance are the company's offices and showrooms. (Michael Stratton)

well-preserved Jewellery Quarter of Birmingham. St Paul's Square was developed as a combination of polite houses and jewellers' premises in the late eighteenth century. Small workshops might be located along narrow plots, with access through wagon arches. From the 1860s local architects used polychromatic brickwork to create Gothic and Italianate façades, in some cases for large factories such as the Albert works (now the Argent Centre) in Frederick Street, built for making pens and pencils in 1863. The layout of a typical late Victorian jewellery workshop can best be appreciated by visiting Smith and Pepper's works in Vyse Street, now the Jewellery Quarter Discovery Centre. The offices were set in the front range, while machinery for stamping and polishing was housed in a top-lit workshop behind. Smelting took place in the cellar. Only a tiny courtyard provided access and lighting, open-air working clearly being inappropriate when handling gold and silver.

Coventry, another centre of precision metalworking, provides the clearest continuity between the traditional workshop and the archetypal twentieth-century factory. Although bombing and comprehensive redevelopment have removed most of the physical evidence, it is possible to identify factories that occupied the central and inner western area of the city in the early twentieth century. The district which exemplifies this transition is West Orchard, which had developed in the medieval period with narrow plots running down to the River Sherbourne. Dyehouses, of which three were established by about 1650, expanded in an *ad hoc* manner, one having grown by 1851 to incorporate several ranges of workshops and two steam engines. An ironworks, the Lion Foundry, was opened following a land purchase in 1833, and also consisted of a cluster of sheds. At this time ribbon-weaving flourished in the area in multi-storey workshops, the earliest of them narrow, tenement-like buildings, in the side streets. Larger factories were built on the meadows fronting the river in the middle years of the century.

Buildings of all sorts were adapted to house the new industries which developed in Coventry during the late nineteenth century. A slump in the ribbon trade from around 1860 made its buildings available, first for cycle manufacture, and when that industry declined in the late 1890s, for making motor cars. One ribbon factory was taken over by Starley & Sutton for cycle manufacture and subsequently occupied by Rover cars. The Lion Foundry was used for making car radiators and other components.

Twentieth-century car and aircraft factories

Most of the car factories of the West Midlands, indeed right across Britain, originated in second-hand buildings and expanded by adaptation and the accretion of further workshops. Single-storey workspaces proved more convenient for making a large, heavy product and for such ancillary processes as metal-pressing and heat treatment. Offices, showrooms and upholstery manufacture might be accommodated in a two-storey block which could provide a respectable street frontage. Early car factories, of which many survive in inner city areas, represent a finely tuned balance between the formal, urban approach to factory layout, and the looser, rurally derived tradition. Calcott Brothers of Coventry developed a works on the eastern fringe of the city to produce cycles and motorcycles from 1905, and cars from 1913. The works, in Far Gosford Street, remains, with its ornate façade of 1896, enlivened by terracotta detailing and Dutch-style gables. The sheds behind, the earliest with timber roof members, and the later additions with steel trusses, are now used by a builders' merchant.

The architectural form of many turn-of-the-century car factories reflected local building traditions. Pioneering motor-car manufacturers in Sheffield occupied narrow buildings akin to the city's cutlery workshops. William Morris was able to take over a redundant college in Oxford, gaining a grandiose setting for the production of the Bullnose Morris, the prototype having been built in 1912 in a workshop at the back of his hire garage in Longwall Street. He used one of the three-storey ranges of the Oxford Military College, which still stands at Cowley on the southern edge of the city, for fabricating the chassis and such components as wheels. Single-storey sheds were erected in the college quadrangle from about 1913, and on adjoining land during World War I (34).

First-generation car producers organized their factories on the workshop system. Each shop was housed in a separate building or a sectioned-off part of a larger block, and was equipped with the machinery and equipment necessary to produce a specific component or sub-assembly. The floor area of the chassis-erecting shop would dictate the number of cars that could be assembled at any one time. Managers struggled to maintain some element of rationality in the layout of their plants as they invested in new erecting shops, saw mills, machine shops and power houses. At Hillman's works at Aldermoor Lane, Coventry, now occupied by Peugeot, the natural slope across the site dictated the basic layout, gravity aiding the transfer of components from the parts store, and of chassis from one shop to the next.

Most car manufacturers gave little attention to architecture as a means of advertising, since the larger Edwardian works, Longbridge in Birmingham, Cowley at Oxford, and Aldermoor Lane in Coventry, were all located in the suburbs, out of the public eye. Only Vauxhall opted to invest in urbane architecture for their new plant on the southern edge of Luton (35). Their office block, which survives, was built in 1907 to the design of H. B. Creswell, in a Queen Anne style, with a pediment above the entrance

adorned with the company's wyvern symbol. Its pilasters and deep red and silver-grey bricks set the tone for other buildings erected facing Kimpton Road, including the showroom and the sales training block.

A more structured approach to the relationship between office, component manufacture and final assembly areas emerged during World War I with investment in plant for making munitions and aeroplanes. The welfare aspects of such factories are considered in

34 The Oxford Military College, designed by T. G. Jackson, built in 1877–8, and taken over by William Morris, later first Lord Nuffield, for car production in 1912. Chassis were assembled on the first floor and car bodies fitted on the second. (RCHME)

35 The office buildings at the Vauxhall factory, Kimpton Road, Luton, showing the corporate style developed by H. B. Creswell. (Michael Stratton)

36 Bodies for Standard Swallow cars being finished in part of a former shell-filling factory in Holbrook Lane, Coventry, built in 1915–16, and taken over by William Lyons in 1928, later to be used for producing Jaguar cars. Note the wooden railway tracks that had been used to trundle filled shells to other parts of the factory. (Jaguar Cars Ltd)

Chapter 1. They are perhaps of greater significance in proving the value and adaptability of large, high, hangar-like sheds, and because they provided the capacity for rapid growth in the car industry in the 1920s and 1930s.

The manufacture of aeroplanes in Britain began during the Edwardian period in such redundant spaces as railway arches and boatyards. The extensive use of wood in early aircraft resulted in the adoption of traditional layouts and practices. Aircraft frames were assembled on trestles alongside saw mills. The growth of production during World War I was made possible by the construction of large A-framed sheds which could accommodate complete aircraft, and permit them to be pushed from one work station to the next as wings, tails, engines and propellers were affixed. Some firms had partitioned-off areas within their main blocks to produce sub-assemblies. Others erected ancillary buildings. The Sopwith Aviation Company took over an old skating rink in Canbury Park Road, Kingston, Surrey in 1912. Their complex developed over the next three years to consist of a three-storey office block, fronting a series of single- and two-storey workshops.

While the Sopwith works produced aircraft until 1960, many other factories were adapted after the armistice to manufacture motor vehicles. In Coventry the Canley works of Standard, developed from 1916 to build fighter planes, was designed around a series of single-storey, A-framed sheds. The largest hangars proved ideal for a moving motor-car assembly line which was installed in 1920. In 1928 William Lyons transferred his coachbuilding workshop from Blackpool to a partly disused shell-filling factory in Holbrook Lane, Coventry, built in 1916 (**36**). It was in these narrow buildings, only two bays wide, that Lyons developed the cars which were ancestors of the Jaguar marque. The sheds, complete with their wood rails for the transport of filled shells, are now occupied by Dunlop Aviation.

Most of the new capacity for the rise in car production during the 1920s and 1930s came from extensions to existing plant, particularly new metal press shops and body-welding areas. The only completely new works was the Ford complex on the Thames Estuary at Dagenham, built in 1929–31 (37). The plant included a jetty, a power station, blast furnaces and a steelmaking plant. Car production was accommodated in one vast partition-less 'flexible shop', with the machine shops in the northernmost bays, and the assembly lines and dispatch bays conveniently close to the river.

Aircraft manufacturers were also faced with the choice of grouping assembly and sub-assembly work in one large building, or dispersing the latter through a series of ancillary structures. By 1930 the de Havilland works at Hatfield, Hertfordshire, had a main production area 210 by 90m (689 by 295ft), in which there was space for sub-assembly areas and a machine shop, as well as an erecting shop laid out for flow production. A similar formula was adopted for the aircraft and aero-engine plants built with government assistance from 1937, mostly on the edges of Coventry and Birmingham. Typically

the plant and services were housed under one roof, with the engine-test cells banished at the far end of the site. As at de Havilland, a stylish two-storey office block was erected in front of each complex. These *shadow* factories, so named because the output of one would 'shadow' another, as a precaution against air-raid damage, were converted to produce motor cars in the late 1940s. Shadow factories are still used for assembling cars by Peugeot at Ryton-on-Dunsmore, and by Jaguar at Browns Lane, both in Coventry, and by Rolls-Royce at Crewe.

Many post-World War II car factories have been located on disused airfields. Sophisticated electric conveyors permit dispersed plans. At the Nissan plant, erected near Sunderland in 1984–6, the building in which final assembly takes place is distinct from the body shop, paint shop and engine-assembly sections, each of which is housed in its own metal-framed and metal-clad building, connected to the assembly line by a covered conveyor. The 'just in time' principle has reduced the need for huge stores to stockpile components and sub-assemblies, while artificial lighting allows most services to be suspended from the roof.

37 An aerial view of the Ford works at Dagenham, built 1929–31. The vast production area is fronted by an office block facing the jetty and the River Thames. To the right can be seen the power station, blast furnaces and coking plant. (Ford Motor Company)

4
Function or fashion?

Why are factories distinctive and yet so different from each other? How do they differ from other buildings? Are they designed by the same architects who built houses, churches, shops and town halls? Do they conform to distinctive architectural styles? Discussions of industrial buildings tend to suppose either that they can be understood purely in terms of the history of architecture, by reference to their style and to the architects who designed them, or that they are simply expressions of their structure and the processes they accommodated, and that they can be understood best in technological terms. This chapter will examine these viewpoints and suggest a synthesis which accommodates the two extremes.

Functional and vernacular

Most discussions of industrial buildings start from the premiss that technology is the factor that distinguishes factories from houses or churches. Factories are regarded as *functional*, suggesting that they were built to last and that they look right because they are un-selfconscious, honest structures. This approach has spread more confusion than enlightenment because the word 'functional' carries at least three distinct meanings. It can be used in a specific sense in the context of the history of architecture, to mean the austere style derived from the Bauhaus in Weimar, which was fashionable until the 1970s, and is otherwise called 'modernist'. The word was also applied

by J. M. Richards and other writers to laud the merits of warehouses, mills and bridges built of brick and iron in the late eighteenth and early nineteenth centuries. In a more literal sense the word has been applied to any building constructed in such a way as to fulfil the purposes for which it was designed by the employment of a minimum quantity of building materials, deployed in structural forms of minimum complexity, without ornamental features. Examples might be a bottle oven, a barn or casting-house.

None of these interpretations of 'functional' is helpful in isolation as a means of understanding the majority of the factories in England. In almost every factory complex there are buildings of different date, status and style. No building or structure can be designed or erected in a vacuum, divorced from contemporary building traditions, whether local or national, and most factories of any scale or pretension involve a self-conscious effort to impress or advertise the credibility of the owner or owning company.

Another potentially useful concept is that of the *vernacular*. This word is applied to buildings that use locally available materials in forms well-proven by established usage. Watermills and lock-keepers' houses that blend in with their surroundings by using stone from the nearest quarry or brick from an estate yard are universally lauded. It is apparent from a cursory look at almost any industrial town that the vernacular link between local geology, building materials and building forms persisted into the twentieth century, even in factories whose owners and architects were conscious of issues of style and corporate identity.

Function and fashion interweave, pulling in opposite directions, or complementing each other. Generous fenestration in a jewellery factory could provide the best possible lighting for precision work, exploit the potential of plate glass and accord with a taste for the Italian Renaissance style. The best way of understanding a seemingly chaotic collection of architectural ephemera is to employ a loose but all-embracing typology which overlays such conventional stylistic classifications as Italianate, Gothic and Baroque, used by historians of architecture.

At the bottom of the scale are buildings and structures which pay conscious attention to neither fashion style nor structural innovations. They may be described as 'work-a-day', 'utilitarian' or, in more academic terms, *sub-idiomatic*. In their materials and construction they are likely to follow prevailing national, regional or local traditions, but sometimes they will seem not even to aspire to conformity with the building stock of the locality. Higher up the scale, and representing a loosely defined median, are buildings that conform to the fashions of contemporary architecture. In form and detail such *idiomatic* buildings follow contemporary tastes for materials and styles, though the choice of a particular strand of Renaissance or Gothic may be influenced as much by regional as by national fashions. At the top of the hierarchy are buildings that were intended to stand above contemporary traditions, many of which were *flagships* which dictated subsequent fashions, although some were disregarded as eccentricities.

The full range – from sub-idiomatic to flagship – can be perceived in every period. Examples from different points on the scale may be found within a single complex, maybe with shacks built from waste materials at the back of the site, carefully detailed idiomatic workshops in the middle, and a dramatic erecting shop or office block providing an impressive frontage. It would be easy to relate the scale to the hierarchy of designers involved, hypothesizing that sub-idiomatic structures would be the work of a builder or would have been thrown up by the factory workers themselves. Architects, especially local practices, are more likely to have been involved in the design of idiomatic buildings. It might be assumed that flagship buildings were always the work of a figurehead architect or engineer, but especially in the pre-Victorian period the designer could have been a local, even an anonymous figure, responding to the ideas of an entrepreneur.

Sub-idiomatic structures

Sub-idiomatic buildings provide space and other necessities for manufacturing, but are unlikely to have been designed to make any conscious architectural statement, which is not to say that they cannot have any aesthetic qualities. Neither is it acceptable to describe them as being mere *building* as opposed to *architecture*.

Such buildings are likely to be located away from public view – on remote moorland, in a mining landscape, in a back street, or screened by other buildings. These work-a-day structures are characteristic of all industries, all parts of the country and all periods. The most ubiquitous form is the single-storey rectangular shed with walls of brick or rubble stone, and a roof of stone, slate or tile supported by rafters and possibly simple trusses. Waste materials, overburnt bricks, kiln saggars and copper slag may be used, occasionally to decorative effect (**38**).

Most ironworks developed as clusters of sheds, casting-houses being set against the walls of the blast furnaces or alongside air furnaces or cupolas (**39**). There was no need for rotative power in all parts of the works, but processes of casting, reheating, hammering and rolling had to take place at ground-floor level. A shed, possibly incorporating iron components in the form of internal columns and beams, could

38 A characteristic sub-idiomatic industrial building, Field Mill, Ramsbottom. The mules, which are ranged on the first floor of the mill, were used until 1988 for spinning cotton yarn. The line-shafting in the mill had been powered by electric motors, from which power was conveyed by means of a rope-drive system since the early twentieth century. The buildings date from the mid-nineteenth century and are of conventional construction, with cast-iron columns and timber cross-beams. (Michael Stratton)

provide the required workspace and protection from the weather. Rooftop louvres or wide openings in the gable ends ensured ventilation from the heat and fumes. An early, and much adapted, example of the ironworking shed survives at the Upper Forge, Coalbrookdale, and is now part of the Ironbridge Gorge Museum. The north-lit shed, whether used for textiles or metalworking, represents a logical evolution of this tradition, with iron columns supporting roof trusses angled to provide steep north lights that prevent direct sunlight and shadows falling on to machinery or workbenches. Most were left unornamented, though their jagged gable ends might be obscured, especially in the twentieth century.

Multi-storey textile mills evolved to have more formal overtones than sheds, partly due to the scale of investment that they represented and their greater physical presence. Ornate, architecturally impressive mills were always in the minority among the mills of a particular region, being the exception to a more modest rule. The silk mills of Macclesfield are often described in terms of their Classical elegance, but only seven of more than forty mills constructed in the town between 1780 and 1832 were 'Palladian' in style (**40**). The remainder, of which some examples survive, were plain structures, rectangular or L-shaped in plan, usually of three storeys, with pitched roofs, and window surrounds which were wholly unornamented. A Scottish flax manufacturer visiting Leeds in 1821 recorded that few mills were fireproof, most being 'old, irregular-looking houses seemingly much disfigured with alterations and additions. Some of the smaller ones are even made out of a range of old dwelling-houses and are extremely mean and inconvenient.'

The industrial structures viewed as being most directly 'functional' are those designed around specific functions, typically those involving heat.

Blast furnaces, bottle ovens, glass cones and limekilns are not 'buildings' in the conventional sense and can rarely be described in terms applicable to country houses, churches or town halls. Stone or brick were carefully worked to create stable structures that could withstand heat – the precise forms and details being determined by operational considerations. In north Staffordshire, pottery kilns have broader bases than those used for calcining flint. All rules are sometimes broken and some kilns and furnaces were ornamented. The smiths' workshops within the retaining wall of the blast-furnace complex at Blists Hill, Ironbridge, are fronted with Gothic arches (**41**), while the bottle ovens at Enoch Wood's Fountain Place pottery at Burslem of 1789 were crenellated.

Idiomatic: mainstream architecture

An idiomatic factory building reflects some conscious effort by the designer to conform to accepted practice. Such a factory could be taken as a median, where forms, style and detailing are influenced by developments and fashions that shape contemporary civic buildings, banks, schools and churches. The design may take its

39 An early twentieth-century view of the ironworks in Coalbrookdale, looking north up the valley, and showing the preponderance of sheds of various dates, grouped around the cupola furnaces where iron was melted. To the north, the largest building in the complex is the erecting shop, beyond which are situated the company's warehouses. The mid-nineteenth-century building in the foreground with nine sections of hipped roof, was used during World War II for the assembly of aircraft wings. (Ironbridge Gorge Museum Trust)

40 Union Mill, Statham Street, Macclesfield, one of the town's elegant 'Palladian' silk factories, built c. 1820, and now demolished. (Barrie Trinder)

41 Gothic ornamentation in an ironworks of the second quarter of the nineteenth century. Behind the masonry bases of the three blast furnaces at Blists Hill, Ironbridge, which are just visible, are three retaining arches. Behind the arches at the upper level are blacksmiths' shops, where tools used in the works were maintained. (Roger Viggers)

cue from other factories as much as from more prestigious buildings built in city centres or for the aristocracy.

The elevations of many industrial buildings follow the architectural idioms of the period when, and of the region where, they were built. The loom houses and carding mills of Saddleworth are in the same tradition of buildings as the farmsteads of the parish but they are also strong architectural statements in their own right with long-light windows and cantilevered external staircases. One of the most distinctive regional industrial buildings is the Cornish engine house. The first 'Cornish' engine, a slow-moving, fuel-efficient, single-cylinder beam engine, was erected by Richard Trevithick at Wheal Prosper mine in 1811. The type was

subsequently used to pump water from almost every mine in the south-western peninsula. Over 300 engine houses survive in Devon and Cornwall. A Cornish engine house is stone-built, rectangular in plan, with a round chimney at one corner and, at the opposite end, a massive 'bob wall' on which the beam rocked (**42**). Two Cornish engines, at East Pool and Taylor's Shaft near Redruth, are displayed to the public.

A Cornish engine house is easily recognized, but other distinctive regional building types fail to be noticed when they cease to serve their original purposes. A four-storey piered building of early nineteenth-century date which forms part of the Stanley Mill complex in Gloucestershire has been admired as a precursor of the International Modern style (**43**). Its construction is certainly interesting, but it is well within the mainstream of Gloucestershire mill buildings. The range is constructed on stone arches set over the tailrace from the main mill, and is nine bays wide, each bay being delineated by ashlar piers which rise the whole height of the building. It is known, from recent use, as the factory's fitters' shop. A similar building of pier-and-panel construction remains at Woodchester Mill, and the German architect Karl Friedrich von Schinkel sketched a building of the type at Wotton-under-Edge in 1826, describing it as having openings filled with a chequered pattern of bricks, forming what he described as *Luftoffnungen* (air openings). It seems therefore that this building, far from being an innovative engineering shop, is a drying-house, similar to others in Gloucestershire mills, which was originally of two storeys, and was subsequently, perhaps when its purpose changed, enlarged with the addition of two further floors.

A distinct regional idiom can be observed in the textile mills of West Yorkshire. Most mills were in stone, although there were brick buildings in Leeds and on the fringe of the coalfield. In stone mills windows had rectangular lintels, in brick mills segmental arches. Ornamentation was usually sparse, and before 1850 was confined to occasional pediments or Diocletian windows in the end walls of attic storeys. The completion of Saltaire Mill in 1853 appears to have marked a turn to the Italianate, which became the accepted regional style.

A more pronounced development of style can be observed in the cotton mills of Lancashire, where brick was the principal building material. In many early nineteenth-century mills stone voussoirs around the wagon arches were the only form of ornamentation. After 1825, however, stone cornices were incorporated on many multi-storey buildings, corners might be ornamented with pilasters, and entrances stressed with rusticated voussoirs or stone pillars. As in Yorkshire, there was a move towards the Italianate style in the 1850s, a precedent being set by Gilnow Mill, Bolton, completed in 1858, which has a six-storey tower, dentilled cornices, string courses, and pairs of pilasters at the corners which also flank important parts of the frontage.

42 Botallack tin mine, Cornwall. This mine, located near St Just, has a remarkable group of Cornish engine houses, the one in the foreground showing the characteristic round chimney at the corner, with the remains of the bob wall to the left. In the distance is a further pumping engine house and the winding engine house which worked a famous diagonal shaft running under the sea. To the right is a headstock forming part of Geevor mine which continued working into the 1990s. (Michael Stratton)

43 A building of pier-and-panel construction at Stanley Mill, Gloucestershire. The building was constructed over the tailrace from the waterwheels of the main mill, presumably after the completion of the latter in 1813, and before the mid-1820s. The building was originally of two storeys, and was probably a drying-house, with wooden louvres between the piers, for which peg holes remain in the stonework. It was subsequently enlarged to four storeys, and for several generations the ground floor was used as a fitters' shop. Similar methods of pier-and-panel construction were used at other Gloucestershire woollen mills, and in the first generation of buildings at the nearby Swindon locomotive works of the Great Western Railway. (Barrie Trinder)

Victorian industrial architecture was influenced by debates over choices of style and materials. Specific forms and styles were deemed appropriate for particular building types and locations. City-centre buildings were expected to be formal in plan and traditional in their choice of material, while the innovative use of decorative ceramics and eclectic styles were acceptable in other locations. In accordance with this code, banks were expected to be stone-built and soberly Classical, but pumping stations might be loosely Italianate or Gothic and make exuberant use of ceramics or cast iron.

Such regional variations in the use of brick and stone were maintained into the twentieth century, and new, industrial vernaculars emerged just when mass production and rail transport might have been expected to promote bland uniformity. The most distinctive regional idiom emerged in lowland Lancashire between 1880 and 1914. A group of architects – the brothers Abraham H. Stott (1822–1904) and Joseph Stott (1837–94) and their sons, Sir Sidney Stott (1858–1937) and George Stott (1876–1936), all of Oldham, George Woodhouse (1827–83), Jonas Bradshaw (1837–1912) and John Gass (1855–1939) – developed the Italianate style of the mid-nineteenth century to take advantage of the opportunities presented by new materials – machine-made bricks fired at high temperatures, terracotta and steel-framing – to create the distinctive Lancashire spinning mill (**44**). Such mills have large windows and restrained ornamentation, early examples having pilasters with sandstone capitals. Most had towers, supporting water tanks for sprinkler systems, which were often ornamented with stone or terracotta detailing, white glazed brick spelling out the name of the mill. The tops of towers might be pyramidal, of mansard shape, or could be capped by copper domes, or in the case of one factory on the edge of Stockport, designed by A. H. Stott & Co. and completed in 1913, in the shape of a pear, the fruit from which the mill takes its name.

Birmingham has no one distinctive building type to compare with the Lancashire spinning mill, but the city does have a distinctive architectural style. More than in most industrial cities Gothic was employed in industrial buildings. A Birmingham architect, J. G. Bland, was largely responsible for establishing the idiom to which most carpet factories in Kidderminster conformed in the second half of the nineteenth century (**45**). At the time that his steam-powered Longmeadow factory was nearing completion in 1854, a local newspaper commented:

In the construction of these buildings a desire has been manifested to make them not only substantial and convenient for the purposes for which they are destined but to render them ornamental to the neighbourhood. Hitherto the custom in Kidderminster has been to erect factories without the slightest

regard to anything but the question how to accommodate a certain quantity of looms or other machinery at the least architectural cost and the result has been the town is filled with lank, plain-walled, ugly-windowed, dismal-looking factories, which, however necessary they may be for its welfare, sadly compromise the respectability of its appearance.

There could be no more eloquent apologia for the idiomatic factory. Kidderminster's carpet mills of the late nineteenth century have red or blue brick walls with simple blocks of stone or contrasting buff brick highlighting window-sills, elevations being topped by dentilled cornices. Stour Vale Mills, also designed by Bland, shows an extensive use of white brick, especially on the engine house. Regional architectural idioms were developed by a small number of architectural practices specializing in commercial and industrial work. Each major provincial city has one or two dominant practices: Joseph Goddard in Leicester,

44 Croal Mill, Bolton, Lancashire, designed by Bradshaw & Gass in 1907. A steam-powered spinning mill with a steel frame, generous use of hard red brick and terracotta, a projecting engine house, and a tower incorporating a water tank and carrying the name of the mill. (Michael Stratton)

45 The Castle Mill at Kidderminster, one of the many mid-nineteenth-century factories in that town designed by J. G. Bland. (Alan Goff)

46 The entrance to Brannam's Pottery in Litchdon Street, Barnstaple, Devon, designed by W. C. Oliver. Most of the nineteenth-century factories in the town follow this idiomatic style, combining buff and red bricks, with doors and windows in apertures set back from the building line. (Michael Stratton)

Thomas Hine in Nottingham, M. E. Hadfield in Sheffield, W. C. Oliver in Barnstaple (**46**). A locally distinct style can be observed in the industrial buildings of many towns. The north-eastern quarter of Kettering, an area which developed rapidly in the 1880s with the growth of the boot and shoe trade, has numerous factories, up to four storeys in height, with cast-iron window-frames, set between projecting brick piers. The detailing tends to be derived from the Baroque style, with broken pediments above porches and the use of swags as decoration.

Flagship architecture

The flagship factory is at the top of the scale. Such a factory was a building of unusual celebrity, larger, employing more workers, having more power available, and deploying more advanced technology than others in its region. Flagship factories are often expressed in flamboyant architectural styles. Their architects and owners intended them to make statements about the place of manufacturing in society. They do not follow past fashions in industrial architecture. They may dictate those of the future.

The first flagship works were built by the government. The Royal Brass Foundry at Woolwich, built in 1715–17, was designed, reputedly, by Sir John Vanbrugh, with a central entrance akin to that of a palace, the doorway topped by a heraldic crest above which is a cupola. The most ostentatious of the first generation of spinning mills employed many of the architectural features of Palladian country houses. An example is Masson Mill at Cromford in Derbyshire built in 1783–4 when Richard Arkwright was rich and famous. It is in brick, with rusticated stone quoins. The central bays of the front elevation are extended to accommodate a staircase and lavatories, and are lit by eight Venetian windows and three Diocletian windows (see **11**).

Stanley Mill is pre-eminent among the woollen mills of Gloucestershire (**colour plate 7**). The manufacture of woollen cloth in the Stroud valley was reorganized on a factory basis in the late eighteenth century and early nineteenth century. Most factories developed around a nucleus, a clothier's mansion, a fulling mill or a warehouse. Almost all were of traditional stone construction. Stanley Mill was built in 1813 by George Harris, Donald Maclean and Charles Stephens on an old watermill site, transformed by the creation of a new five-acre (2ha) pool on land which had been acquired piecemeal from 1810. The principal building has an elaborate iron frame, apparently designed to accommodate three sets of line-shafting, yet it is doubtful whether power was initially used in all parts of the building. The architectural detailing is of exceptional quality. The building is mainly of brick, although the ground floor is partially of finely rusticated stone, and it has stone quoins throughout. Ornate, iron-framed rose windows form fanlights above the entrances. The central bays of the principal elevation, to the north, have Venetian windows. The waterwheels at Stanley Mill provided more power, some 200hp, than was available in any other Gloucestershire mill. Its labour-force was larger than at any other mill, and by 1840 it was the only textile factory in Gloucestershire to be lit by gas. A poet in 1824 lauded it as the largest mill in the county. Visitors to Gloucestershire, whether parliamentary commissioners, or the Prussian architect Karl Friedrich von Schinkel, sought to visit Stanley. Iron columns and discs divide the ground floor into compartments, in each of which there was a waterwheel driving a set of fulling stocks. The whole floor seems to have been designed to allow the machinery to be admired, just as in the eighteenth century some blast furnaces in France had galleries for privileged spectators. The mill was built at a time when manufacturers felt threatened by Luddite riots, and it can be interpreted as a declaration of the values of the factory system.

It can equally be seen as a statement that gentlemen clothiers could create buildings as impressive as the stately homes of Gloucestershire's gentry. Stanley Mill and Staverton Mill, its Wiltshire equivalent, show that some factories were not 'utilitarian' or 'functional' structures. They were buildings in which the language of architecture was employed to make statements of the same kind as those conveyed by town halls, castles, churches or art galleries (**47**). Quarry Bank Mill on the River Bollin at Styal was begun by the Ulsterman Samuel Greg in 1783. The first building was of five storeys, eighteen bays long, with a pediment surmounted by a clock and a cupola over the three central bays. The mill complex was steadily expanded, until by the 1840s it was one of the largest in the region, a succession of plain but elegant buildings,

47 Staverton Mill, near Trowbridge, Wiltshire, whose rebuilding after a fire in 1823 was commemorated by the phoenix on the pediment. The woollen mill was converted to a milk condensery in 1897–8 by the Anglo-Swiss Condensed Milk Co. The top four storeys were demolished in the 1930s. The picture shows motor lorries delivering churns of milk to the factory *c.* 1920. (Nestlé International)

celebrated for its huge 120hp waterwheel, 9.75m (32ft) in diameter and 7.3m (24ft) wide. It was much visited, and formed part of a landscape designed to encourage a contented work-force.

The flagship of the Yorkshire worsted industry was Saltaire Mill (**colour plate 8**), built on a rural site on the River Aire north of Bradford by Titus Salt, a successful millowner who had been contemplating retirement in 1851, but determined instead to create a model industrial community around a gigantic mill. The building was 170m (557ft) long, which was frequently declared to be the same length as St Paul's Cathedral. Its two steam engines developed 1250hp. The mill provided employment for 4500 people. It was of fireproof construction, with a magnificent roof of composite trusses of cast iron and wrought iron. It stood within a community designed to create a contented labour-force, but on a larger scale than at Quarry Bank Mill. The principal chimney, in the form of an Italian campanile, was 76m (208ft) tall, just higher than the Monument in the City of London. The mill expressed many passions in Victorian society, such as the perceived superiority of the manufacturing north of England over the metropolis, and the self-confidence of Nonconformists in their rivalry with the Church of England. The mayor of Bradford declared when the mill was opened in 1853 that his generation had built 'palaces of industry equal to the palaces of the Caesars'.

The flagship of the Yorkshire linen industry was completed some years earlier. Temple Mill formed part of the flax-spinning complex on the south side of Leeds, developed by John Marshall (1765–1845) from 1791. Marshall was a partner in the Ditherington Mill, Shrewsbury, the first iron-framed building, and several buildings on the Leeds site built between 1800 and 1830 were similarly iron-framed, but usually they were of brick construction and lacked ornamentation. Temple Mill, built in 1838–41 and designed by the architect Ignatius Bonomi, was extraordinarily different, a single-storey building in ashlar stone, top-lit with conical lanterns, its roof support on iron columns carrying groined brick vaults. In technological terms it was an innovative design, a huge shed accommodating an integrated linen-producing operation, with facilities for preparation, spinning, twisting thread and weaving cloth. The architectural style was Egyptian. The front elevation of the main building was divided up by eighteen flare-topped columns, beneath a deep cornice, in the centre of which was a representation of an eagle. The office block, which screened the boiler house from the street, was a similar structure of seven bays. Even the steam engine had six Egyptian-style columns in cast iron supporting the cylinders.

Exuberant architecture was also a feature of transport systems. Many large city railway termini were built to create impressions, the first generation to persuade the public that railway travel was safe; the second to show the eminence of particular companies. Of the first the outstanding examples were Philip Hardwick's stations at either end of the London and Birmingham Railway, opened in 1838. Euston, with its Doric arch and its Great Hall, was destroyed in the 1960s, but the main building of Hardwick's Curzon Street station in Birmingham is now used as offices. Its four Ionic columns, heavy entablature and carefully worked ashlar stone, suggest that it was owned by a respectable concern which would provide customers with a safe journey. St Pancras station in London, the single-arch train shed built to the design of W. H. Barlow in 1865–8, and its adjoining hotel designed by George Gilbert Scott and completed in 1876, have aroused stronger emotions than any other station. The station has many of the characteristics of a flagship building. It was the largest construction of its kind when it was built. It was imitated at Manchester Central, Liverpool Central, Glasgow St Enoch and Antwerp Central. It was a defiant statement by the provincially based Midland Railway that it was established in London, and that it intended to compete with other companies by offering a new image of travel, fast and comfortable trains, a huge unencumbered space in which to dismount from them, and a luxuriously appointed hotel in which to rest afterwards.

House style

The concept of house style – the consistent use of a particular architectural idiom to give identity to the buildings of a particular company – emerges from the use of architecture as advertising, first consciously seen in flagship structures. The corporate house style has its origins in the tollhouses constructed by turnpike trusts from the mid-eighteenth century. The Ludlow trust, for example, built tollhouses in the form of two-storey octagonal towers with single-storey wings, sometimes in brick, sometimes in stone, but always with the same chevron-shaped stone lintels, and a recess for the tollboard above the door. When the road from London to Holyhead was improved at government expense after 1815, Thomas Telford produced two designs for tollhouses, one for use between Shrewsbury and the Welsh coast, the other for the final stretch on Anglesey.

Canal and railway companies similarly developed house styles. John Rennie's elegant stone-arched bridges, many of which are visible from the M6 motorway, provide a clear identity for the Lancaster Canal, while farms divided by the Oxford Canal are joined by wooden bascule bridges, and byways on the mosses of north Shropshire cross the Ellesmere Canal on lifting bridges with lofty wooden frames. The stations of the North Staffordshire Railway were built in brick in a Jacobean style to the design of the architect H. A. Hunt.

Entrepreneurs adopted corporate styles when and where they had groups of buildings or complexes in the public domain (**48**). The motivation might be economic or idealistic. Bass of Burton-on-Trent achieved a broad consistency in its breweries and its maltings through entrusting their design to an in-house

48 An example of company house style – the can-making plant at the Staverton works, Trowbridge, built *c.* 1913, by which time the site was owned by the Nestlé company, who constructed buildings of this type, with stepped gables, in high-quality brickwork, at dairy complexes in several parts of England. (Barrie Trinder)

engineer, William Canning, who used red brick and iron window-frames, and wall surfaces with projecting piers topped by round-headed arches both for breweries in the town and for the vast maltings complex at Sleaford, Lincolnshire, built between 1899 and 1905. The resultant economies of construction were complemented by the visual advantages of having a family of well-designed buildings to be illustrated in advertisements.

Co-operative and corporate architecture

The Co-operative movement occupied an important place in British society in the late nineteenth century and early twentieth century, and was responsible both for flagship factories and warehouses, and for the development of corporate house styles. From small beginnings in the 1840s, it became a powerful force in retailing, and a major manufacturer of consumer goods. The Co-operative Wholesale Society was formed in 1863 to supply quality products to retail societies. In the decades which followed it opened factories making footwear, clothing, biscuits and soap. The society's imposing warehouses in central Manchester epitomized its respectability and the collective power of its members, but its flagship factory was the Wheatsheaf boot and shoe works on the southern edge of Leicester, opened in 1891 (**49**). It consisted of a quadrangle of three-storey buildings, each side of which comprised twenty-four bays in a style which mixed Flemish Gothic with Italianate. The steam engines and boilers were housed in a detached group of buildings, beneath a tall chimney. A corner tower was added to the main elevation after 1900. The pride which the society took in the building is conveyed in a description of 1900, which called it:

> one of the grandest monuments of Co-operative enterprise … Here, just where the town of Leicester melts into its open, beautifully green pastures, stands the finest boot and shoe factory in the whole world. The outward appearance of the structure is imposing, and combined with its noble proportions there is a lightness, an airiness, and a brightness about the whole place that is

49 The Wheatsheaf works off Welford Road, Leicester, one of the flagship factories of the Co-operative Wholesale Society, which once provided employment for over 2000 workers. (*CWS Yearbook*, 1909, CWS Library and Information Service)

almost unknown in ordinary factories. Here we have a grand combination of sweetness, light and industry, and a wonderland of machinery.

Corporate architecture proved particularly appropriate for organizations which tried to promote community values. From the time of the establishment of the London Passenger Transport Board in 1933, Charles Holden designed a series of underground stations with sharply defined brick forms, concrete canopies and modern signage to denote efficiency with a human face. He followed Dutch precedents in developing a flexible brand of modernism, as did the designers of the pithead baths commissioned in the 1930s by the Miners' Welfare Fund.

Power stations

It might be expected that the new industries of the twentieth century – electricity generation, plastics, cars and aircraft – would be concentrated in stylish factories. But in practice, new technologies were often developed in modest, even second-hand buildings. Prematurely ambitious buildings could turn out to be 'white elephants'. Only when new ventures

LEICESTER WHEATSHEAF BOOT AND SHOE WORKS.

were well developed could flagship complexes and corporate house styles be justified. This sequence can be seen most clearly in the architecture of power stations. The first generating stations built during the 1880s were modest in scale and style. The first flagship generating station, built by Sebastian Ziani de Ferranti at Deptford 1890–1, was a technological disaster. Over the next thirty years power stations, typically located close to railways, canals or harbours, were often designed in mainstream, idiomatic styles.

Increased demand, larger turbo-alternators and the creation of joint electricity authorities justified the erection of large 'super stations' feeding into regional grids and, from 1933, into the national grid. These 'super stations' – Ironbridge 'A' (1933), Clarence Dock (1931) in Liverpool, and Battersea (1933) in London – were the successors to the flagship mills of the previous century. The 'Saltaire' of electricity generation was Battersea, the first part of which came into operation in June 1933 (50). A commemorative stone was unveiled on St George's Day 1931, the year of the centenary of Michael Faraday's discovery of electromagnetic induction. Its inscription acknowledged that the building was 'a landmark in the development of larger London's light and power and to serve as another memorial of the scientific heritage derived from famous Englishmen'. The detailed external design of the power station was the responsibility of Sir Giles Gilbert Scott, an architect already celebrated as the architect of Liverpool Cathedral. It was the largest unit generating electric power in Europe at the time, and claimed world records in efficiency. It was compared with the Cunard liner *Queen Mary*, which had just achieved the fastest crossing of the Atlantic, and was said to be 'perpetually in London's eye and is on the way to becoming a national symbol'. A former manager claimed, with some exaggeration, that:

50 Turbine Hall A at Battersea Power Station, London, designed by Halliday & Agate and built between 1930 and 1935. The external form of the building was determined by Sir Giles Gilbert Scott. (CEGB Archive)

It was about the first station that got away from the corrugated iron era. It wasn't only its exterior features. The control room was all panelled out with Italian marble, with indirect lighting and polished hardwood parquet flooring, and you weren't allowed to walk in there unless you put felt overshoes on.

Factory buildings cannot be understood without some knowledge of the technological processes they were designed to contain. Equally they should not be seen as 'essentially functional and utilitarian buildings'. Many were built to make architectural statements, whether of conformity, like the factories we have categorized as 'idiomatic', or of assertion, like those we have described as 'flagship' structures. Architects and factory owners rarely confessed their motivations. Sometimes, as at Saltaire or the Wheatsheaf Boot & Shoe factory, they are reasonably self-evident. At Stanley Mill and elsewhere they remain, for the present, the subject of surmise.

5
Strength, span and security

Factories fulfil several basic functions, so their structure is of critical importance. Each building has to provide an unbroken workspace of a particular area depending on the process and product involved. The structure will have to support a roof and often overhead cranes or upper storeys. Furnaces, spark-inducing machinery and flammable materials may make the prevention of fire a major concern. These, and such associated factors as lighting, ventilation, access and power transmission, make the nature of a building structure a key issue in the form of the factory. Studies of the subject have tended to be preoccupied with technological firsts, highpoints and eccentricities, to the neglect of the typical, and of the requirements of entrepreneurs and managers.

Brick and timber were the prime building materials for factories almost until the end of the Victorian period. Humble brickwork, except where suitable clay was not available, was cheap, easy to work, durable and allowed for relatively high walls of modest thickness and, with wooden or stone lintels, wide windows openings. In the twentieth century brickwork has continued to be used for thinner, non-load-bearing walls. Timber, often Baltic softwood, was the ideal complement for window-frames, floors and roof members, again being easy to work and handle. Heavy section beams and posts have proved more durable than more modern materials in many circumstances and

could be readily cut, re-erected or extended as buildings were adapted to new uses. Saw mills, often steam-powered, were established in most towns by the early nineteenth century. Their circular saws, and planing, mortising and moulding machines, brought economies of scale, as well as encouraging the use of ornately carved woodwork.

Andrew Yarranton, a visionary writing in the 1670s who was concerned to see England's economy developed in ways which would set the poor to work and outdo the Dutch, recommended the construction of granaries and manufactories for linen at nodal points in the transport system (51). His seven-storey granaries were to be 300ft (91m) long, 18ft (5.5m) wide, and 49ft (15m) high. Yarranton's sketches of these buildings show that they resembled the ranks of tall, gabled warehouses which line the harbours of the prosperous Dutch ports of this period, such as the Kuiperhavn at Dordrecht.

Buildings designed for manufacturing appear to derive from a different tradition. The first large building in England designed for production was the silk mill at Derby constructed by John Lombe in 1721 (see 6) to house twelve Italian-style circular throwing machines, which occupied ground and first floors, and twenty-six winding machines on the floors above. The main building, the 'Italian works', was of five storeys and was approximately 33.5m (110ft) long, 12m (39ft)

1 Shore Mill, Delph, of *c.* 1780, showing the 'cottage chimney' which indicates that wool-carders probably lived at the mill. (Barrie Trinder)

2 Ruddington Framework Knitting Museum near Nottingham, showing a two-storey frame shop of the period in the early nineteenth century when the manufacture of knitted fabrics dictated the need for larger premises than those used when only stockings were manufactured. (Barrie Trinder)

3 'Arkwright's Mill at Cromford' by Joseph Wright of Derby (1734–97), expressing the artist's amazement at a large building which remained working and illuminated throughout the night. (Derby Museums & Art Gallery)

4 Machinery driven by belts from line-shafting at Stott Park Bobbin Mill. (Barrie Trinder)

5 The engine at Trencherfield Mill, Wigan, a typical Lancashire mill engine of the early twentieth century, which drove spinning machines in the mill by means of ropes from the flywheel. (Michael Stratton)

6 The chimney at the end of the lengthy flue at Allendale, Northumberland, by which noxious fumes from the Allendale lead smelter were conveyed to the moors on the hillside above. (Michael Stratton)

7 Interior of the first floor of Stanley Mill, Gloucestershire, built in 1813, showing the elaborate iron frame capable of accommodating three sets of line-shafting, although it is doubtful whether such shafting was ever installed. (Michael Stratton)

8 Saltaire Mill, the flagship of the Yorkshire worsted industry, built in 1853. (Barrie Trinder)

9 The Long Shop, the erecting shop of Richard Garrett & Co., engineers, of Leiston, Suffolk, erected in 1853. (Barrie Trinder)

10 One of the lengthy erecting shops at the Horwich locomotive works of the Lancashire and Yorkshire Railway, built in the mid-1880s. (Michael Stratton)

11 Cross Street and the Green at W. H. Lever's model industrial settlement at Port Sunlight. (Barrie Trinder)

12 The interior of the Wet Processes Building designed for Boots of Nottingham by Sir Owen Williams. (Michael Stratton)

13 The grandiose street frontage of the Clement-Talbot car factory, built in west London, 1903–4. The architect, William T. Walker, faced a structure of reinforced concrete in red brick and Portland stone. (Michael Stratton)

14 The Art Deco frontage of the Hoover building, Perivale, London, 1932. (Michael Stratton)

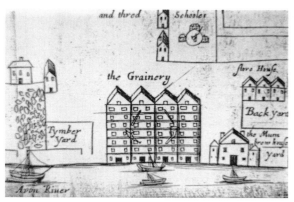

51 Industrial buildings imagined: the granary, brewery, storehouse and timber yard of the town of New Brunswick, which Andrew Yarranton proposed to erect near Stratford-upon-Avon in the 1670s. (From Andrew Yarranton, *England's Improvement by Sea and Land*, London: Everingham, 1677, RSA Library, London)

wide and 17m (56ft) high. Few constructional details are known but the upright columns and cross-beams would certainly have been of timber. The width was greater than that of most of the first generation of cotton mills. The precedents for the main building, as the name suggests, were probably in Italy, but while the origins of Lombe's circular throwing machines have been competently investigated, the prototypes of the buildings constructed at Derby have yet to be identified.

The structure of Richard Arkwright's mill at Cromford completed in 1771 set the pattern for most large-scale cotton-spinning factories for the century which followed. The mill had load-bearing stone walls, and an internal structure of wooden upright columns carrying wooden beams, on which rested the joists carrying the floor above. The first generation of water-powered cotton mills was usually of three or four storeys, about 22m (72ft) long and 9m (29½ft) wide, dimensions suited to the arrangement of twin ranks of water frames or carding engines. Extra capacity was achieved by constructing additional storeys. Woollen mills and silk mills of the late eighteenth century and the early nineteenth century were of similar dimensions. Surviving examples of this period

include Masson Mill at Cromford (see **11**), Haarlem Mill, at Wirksworth, Derbyshire, and the Old Mill at Fazeley, Staffordshire.

Iron and fireproofing

Textile machines create flammable dust, and textile mills have always been prone to damage by fire. The first motivation for moving away from wooden construction appears to have been the desire to make mills fireproof. William Strutt was the first to use iron components for this purpose. In 1792–3 he constructed a cotton mill at Derby in which brick arches sprang from substantial timber beams which were supported by cast-iron columns with the unbalanced horizontal thrusts restrained by wrought-iron tie rods. Over the next two years he built two similar buildings: a small warehouse within the mill complex at Milford, and the six-storey, 61m (200ft) long West Mill at Belper. All these buildings have been demolished.

The first wholly iron-framed building was the Ditherington Flax Mill in Shrewsbury, built in 1796–7 (**52**). It was designed by Charles Bage for a partnership which included John Marshall, the pioneer of mechanized flax spinning in Yorkshire, and Thomas and Benjamin Benyon of Shrewsbury, who were also Marshall's partners in his Leeds enterprises. Bage had grown up in Derbyshire, knew William Strutt, and was acquainted with William Reynolds and other pioneering ironmasters of the Coalbrookdale area, although before 1796 he gained his living as a wine merchant and land surveyor. He had a profound knowledge of the structural properties of iron, and was fascinated by the potential of brick vaulting. The mill is 54m (177ft) long and 12m (39ft) wide. Three lines of cruciform columns carry iron cross-beams from which spring brick jack arches sustaining the floors above. Each beam was cast in two halves which abut to the east of the central columns. The half-beams are bolted together through flanges, in the faces of which are semicircular grooves, 5cm (2in) in diameter, through which shafts passed to power machinery on the floors above.

52 The fourth floor of the Ditherington Flax Mill, designed by Charles Bage and built in 1796–7, the first wholly iron-framed building. The three ranks of cruciform cast-iron columns support iron cross-beams, the spaces between which are spanned by brick arches. Line-shafting ran through the spaces at the top of the columns in the central line. This floor was used for the carding of the finer fibres of flax, which were spun on the floor below. The building was used for flax spinning for ninety years, then, after a period of disuse, was converted to a maltings, and was used for that purpose until 1987. (Barrie Trinder)

Ditherington Mill set a pattern which was followed in a significant minority of textile factories for more than sixty years. Within fifteen years cylindrical columns had replaced those of cruciform section. In 1830 a design for a standardized pattern of beam was published by Eaton Hodgkinson. After much experimentation new forms of iron roof structures were designed. Nevertheless the essential features of Ditherington – iron columns and iron beams sustaining brick jack arches, between load-bearing masonry walls, beneath a roof of iron construction – can also be observed in Saltaire Mill, regarded as the epitome of best practice when it was completed in 1853 (**53**).

It has become the convention to describe mills of this type as fireproof, and proof against conflagration was certainly one of the reasons for the use of iron and brick, and the virtual exclusion of timber. The term 'fireproof' appears first to

have been used in this context in a description of Ditherington Mill published in a Shrewsbury newspaper in September 1797. Nevertheless the word can be misleading. Buildings constructed in this way were not immune from fire. Stanley Mill in Gloucestershire was severely damaged by a conflagration in 1884, which accounts for the lines of cylindrical columns which replaced the original iron structural members in some parts of the building, and for the present conventional timber roof. Later forms of construction in steel and concrete, more resistant to fire than buildings of the Ditherington pattern, are not, by convention, described as fireproof.

Fireproofing was probably not the only reason why iron-framed construction was adopted in textile mills of the early nineteenth century. There seems a clear correlation between iron-framing and the manufacture of flax. Table 1 below lists all the principal iron-framed buildings in textile complexes in Britain built in the twenty

53 The same principles of construction used at Ditherington were employed in Upper Tean Mill, Staffordshire, designed by George Augustus Lee in 1823 to accommodate powered tape-weaving looms. Cast-iron beams from which spring brick jack arches run across between the load-bearing walls of the mill, but the cast-iron columns which sustain them are of round not cruciform section. (Michael Stratton)

years after the completion of Ditherington Mill. Fourteen out of the twenty-six were concerned with flax manufacture, a high proportion for a relatively small sector of the textile industry.

Table 1: The first generation of iron-framed factories – the principal textile mill buildings constructed between 1796 and 1816. Those listed in bold are still standing.

1796–7	**Main mill, Ditherington, Shrewsbury**	Flax
1799–1802	Salford Twist Mill	Cotton
1802–3	Main mill, Benyons' Mill, Leeds	Flax
1802–3	Hackling block, Benyons' Mill, Leeds	Flax
1803–4	**North Mill, Belper**	Cotton
1803–4	Castlefields Mill, Shrewsbury	Flax
1804–5	**Flax warehouse, Ditherington**	Flax
1804–6	Houldsworth's Mill, Glasgow	Cotton
1805	**Armley Mill, Leeds**	Woollens
1806	**Warehouse, Marshall's Mill, Leeds**	Flax
1806–7	Bell Mill, Dundee	Flax
1808	Kennedy's Mill, Manchester	Cotton
1808	**Old Mill, Broadford Mill, Aberdeen**	Flax
1809	**Barracks Mill, Whitehaven**	Flax
1811	Greenholme Mill, Burley-in-Wharfedale	Cotton
1811–12	**Hackling block, Ditherington**	Flax
1811–12	South Mill, Belper	Cotton
1812	Wing Mill, Grandholm Works, Aberdeen	Flax
1813	**Stanley Mill, Gloucestershire**	Woollens
1813–20	Chepstow Street Mill, Manchester	Cotton
1814	**Block at Chorlton New Mill, Manchester**	Cotton
1814	**Old Factory, Stakesby Vale, Whitby**	Flax
1815	Otley Mill	Woollens
1815–16	**Mill C, Marshall's Mill, Leeds**	Flax
1816	**Lawrence Street Mill, York**	Flax
1816	Old Rutherglen Road Mill, Glasgow	Cotton

NOTE: This table includes multi-storey buildings with iron upright columns, iron cross-beams, floors made up of stone slabs or brick jack arches, and roofs which were substantially iron-framed. Some small buildings are omitted.

It seems that iron-framed construction was close to being the norm for purpose-built, steam-powered flax mills in the early nineteenth century. No large flax mills of conventional construction appear to have been built in this period. It is possible that iron-framing was used because particularly heavy machinery was used in flax spinning. Iron frames and brick arches may have been avoided in other sectors because they created a humid atmosphere that was detrimental to cotton and wool, but not to flax spinning. Whatever the reason, the adoption of iron-framing in the cotton and wool sectors of the textile industry was slow. The proportion of iron-framed mills before the 1850s was small, and most such mills were exceptional structures in some way. The great majority of textile mills, and indeed of all industrial buildings of similar dimensions, continued to have load-bearing masonry walls, with internal structures and roof trusses of conventional timber construction.

Design by calculation

Nevertheless the technology of iron construction developed during the first half of the nineteenth century, and was increasingly based on scientific calculations. The basis of all subsequent structural use of iron was laid in 1830 when the Manchester Literary and Philosophical Society published Eaton Hodgkinson's *Theoretical and Experimental Researches to Ascertain the Strength and Best Forms of Iron Beams*. Hodgkinson devised a form of I-section beam with equal flanges at top and bottom which is to be found in most mid-nineteenth-century iron-framed buildings. The first use of the beam was in the bridge which carried the Liverpool and Manchester Railway over Water Street in Manchester. The principal advocate of the Hodgkinson beam was William Fairbairn (1789–1874), millwright and engineer of Manchester, who by the 1830s was the most celebrated designer of mills in Britain. It was he who, in 1851–3, was responsible for the construction of Saltaire Mill, although the architectural details were entrusted to the architects Lockwood & Mawson.

Satisfactory forms of iron roof for industrial buildings were also developed in the first half of the nineteenth century. Ditherington Mill has a unique roof structure, with beams supported by a single line of columns, sloping from the crown

54 Fazeley Mill, Fazeley, near Tamworth, constructed for the tape-weavers William Tolson Ltd in 1886, a steam-powered, five-storey structure, with six-bay north and south elevations, and twenty-nine-bay east and west elevations. The mill is a typical composite structure of the late nineteenth century with a central line of cast-iron columns supporting north–south beams of cast iron, and H-section east–west beams of wrought iron, on which rest wooden floorboards. Much of the line-shafting is still in place, although this section of the mill is used only for storage. (Michael Stratton)

of the roof to the tops of the walls, and carrying jack arches of small radius, above which slates were laid, possibly on wooden battens. Most subsequent early nineteenth-century iron-framed mills had roof structures made up of castings which either formed arches, or followed the pattern of conventional wooden rafters, tie beams and purlins. Gradually forms of composite truss were devised, in which castings were used for the members in compression and wrought iron for those in tension (**54**).

What was learned in designing factories in the eight decades between the first part of Arkwright's Cromford Mill and the commencement of building at Saltaire has been of consequence in many fields of human endeavour. The development of the multi-storey iron-framed building, designed according to scientific principles, can be seen as a heroic saga but most factories were not iron-framed. Most industrial buildings were designed to accommodate particular technological processes, not to open up new structural frontiers. In the narrow context of the textile industry, the development of the unheroic north-lit shed from the 1820s was as important as the refinement of techniques of building multi-storey, iron-framed factories.

Steel frames

The introduction of modern materials into British industrial architecture was drawn-out and similarly unheroic. Steel and concrete were adopted fitfully around the turn of the century. Only a few buildings, mostly dating from the inter-war period, show any dramatic exploitation of the architectural potential of metal girders or reinforced concrete. Entrepreneurs, architects and engineers were wary about venturing into areas of structural uncertainty, and were further discouraged by the time that could be lost in arguing with local authority officers. Adoption of the two materials often went hand in hand. Steel rods and bars were used to reinforce the gravel, sand and cement of concrete. Steel beams and columns frequently supported floors of reinforced concrete.

The trainshed of St Pancras station, London, erected in 1866–8, with its soaring 74m (243ft) span, was both the culmination and the swan-song of the use of wrought iron in British architecture. In 1856 Henry Bessemer had made steel on a large scale by blowing air through molten pig-iron in a converter, and in the following decade William Siemens and others developed the alternative open-hearth process. Thus by the 1870s architects and engineers had available mild steel, a new material with strength in both tension and compression.

Several decades elapsed before steel was accepted for engineering structures, and still longer before it was used for buildings. The Board of Trade only recognized it as a suitable material for bridges in 1877, and the material was initially viewed with caution by the civil engineering profession. Quality could not be assured. Nevertheless the completion in 1890 of the Forth railway bridge, with two huge 521m (1709ft) long cantilevered spans, demonstrated the potential of steel. The Brooklyn Bridge, New York, opened in 1883, showed the strength of steel in tension. Most of the first generation of skyscrapers in Chicago, like the six upper floors of the ten-storey Home Insurance Building of 1885, designed by William Le Baron Jenney, had lightweight frames of Bessemer steel.

The basic component of most steel structures – the H-section (or I-section) beam – was being advertised across Britain in the mid-1880s. One of the most important suppliers, Dorman Long of Teesside, found that their steel girders were often used for horizontal floor beams, which were supported by traditional cast-iron columns. This combination was specified in 1884 by Potts, Pickup & Dixon for their Palm Mill in Oldham. By the middle of the following decade steel girders were also being used for columns, the complete frame being bolted or riveted together. A furniture warehouse in West Hartlepool, Robinson's Emporium of 1896–8, is recognized as the first completely steel-framed building to be erected in Britain. It was built by Basil Scott of the engineering firm, Redpath, Brown & Co. The Great Northern Railway warehouse in Manchester, also completed in 1898 (see Chapter 7), also has a riveted steel frame between its thick external walls (55).

The steel girder was widely accepted by 1900, but as just one component in the hybrid structures of such large buildings as banks and hotels, and only where a wide span was needed, as over hallways or bay windows. Steel joists were incorporated within the extensions added to the Savoy Hotel, London, about 1896, each member being wrapped in brick or terracotta to protect it from rust and fire. When another London hotel, the Ritz, was built in 1904–5, with a complete steel frame, its engineer, Sven Bylander, still had to specify thick, load-bearing walls to meet London County Council regulations. It was only in 1909 that the LCC

55 Detail of the riveted steel frame of the Great Northern Warehouse, Manchester, of 1895–8. (Michael Stratton)

accepted that the external walls of steel-framed buildings should not necessarily be regarded as load-bearing.

Steel had gained broad acceptance by 1914, and during World War I it proved invaluable for the erection of aircraft factories and hangars, giving spans of up to 45m (148ft) and unobstructed door openings up to 84m (276ft) wide. Girders and light-section roof trusses became the norm for inter-war industrial sheds. A north-lit shed was likely to be built on concrete foundations with H-section steel columns supporting the roof members. More sophisticated frames could be fabricated, aided by welding and high-strength bolts (56).

Ferro-concrete

Concrete was first used in Britain in mass form – without reinforcement – in docks in London during the early 1800s. Mass concrete consists of cement, sand and a stone aggregate. It is strong in compression but weak in tension, and hence of little use for a beam which tends to stretch along its bottom edge. The solution to this problem was to embed metal into such beams. An essential prelude was the invention of Portland cement, which was patented in 1824, and made by

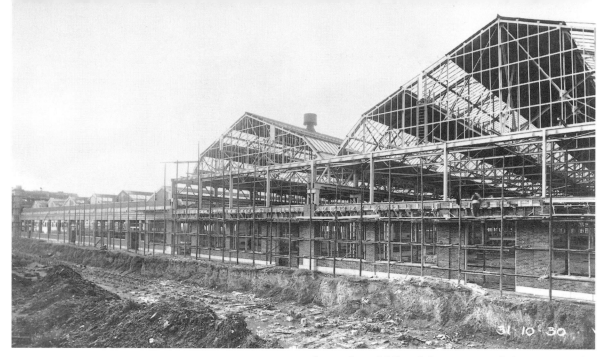

56 A photograph dated 31 October 1930 showing the part-completed Dagenham factory of the Ford Motor Co., designed by Charles Heathcote & Sons. The structure is completely of steel, with brick being applied as a superficial cladding. (Ford Motor Co.)

burning clay and limestone together. It created a strong concrete and also proved to have a preservative effect on corrodible metalwork. Several patents were taken out in Britain in the 1850s for concrete reinforced with wrought iron, but they were not exploited, and it was a group of French engineers who recognized that steel offered greater strength in tension than wrought iron, and was potentially more useful as a means of reinforcing concrete.

Concrete interested industrialists and their engineers because it could be cheaper than a steel frame. It was also fireproof, so that it did not need to be encased with tile or plaster. British architects and engineers first exploited the potential of concrete for floors. One of the first uses was in a private asylum built near Bristol in the 1830s. The engineer responsible, Henry Fox, teamed up with a builder, James Barrett. Their *Fox & Barrett* floor, with wrought-iron joists embedded in layers, from bottom to top, of mortar, concrete and lime and sand, was used in hospitals and office buildings

from the middle of the century. Other patented systems were tried, but none could offer the wide spans and simple construction needed for factories.

It was only when more sophisticated forms of lightweight reinforcement had been developed that concrete floors became widely used in industry. Concrete was sometimes chosen as a substitute for brick-arch systems in the 1890s, but in most textile mills, especially in the West Riding, concrete was employed to encase steel beams rather than as a substitute for them. Falcon Mill, Handel Street, Bolton, built by Bradshaw & Gass in 1904, was hailed as a pioneering example of a factory with flooring of reinforced concrete, in which slabs 0.1–0.15m (4–6in) thick were reinforced with steel rods to take tensional strains. During the Edwardian period full concrete framing, embracing beams, floors, columns and even staircases, came to be used in Britain. This architectural revolution was dependent on experiments in France and America.

A French gardener, Joseph Monier, patented a form of reinforced beam in 1849, and in the 1870s began to make huge water tanks strengthened by vertical and horizontal rods. At the same time François Coignet promoted the use of concrete for the façades of apartment

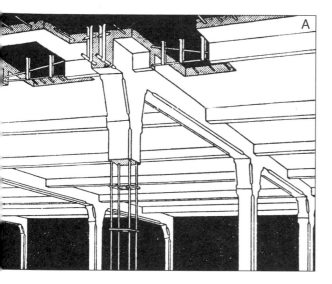

57 A: Cutaway of the Mouchel-
Hennebique system of reinforced concrete
construction. It shows the form of beam
and column reinforcement, and the
relationship between main bars and
stirrups. Patented in 1897, this system was
used for Britain's earliest reinforced
concrete buildings.
B: The Kahn system of reinforced concrete
construction, showing the simpler
reinforcing bar. Patented in 1903 in the
USA, it was used widely in Britain for both
columns and beams from *c.* 1907.
(*Rivington's Notes on Building
Construction*, 1930, figs 294 and 296)

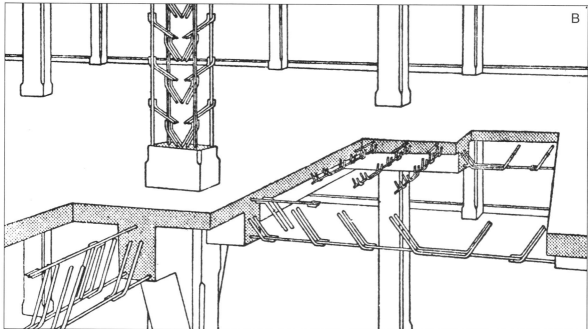

blocks. A stonemason turned contractor,
François Hennebique, took out several patents
in the 1890s. He set bars near to the undersides
of concrete beams, with others sloping to rise
close to the top at the point where the beams sat
on columns (57). These two sets of bar were
joined by slim U-shaped straps or stirrups which
countered shear strains. His ferro-concrete
columns might be square, circular or polygonal
in section, with steel reinforcement or rods
secured at intervals by steel binding wire. He

advocated concrete frames that allowed
lightweight infill panels, primarily of glass, to be
substituted for brick or masonry walls.

Hennebique successfully marketed concrete
construction across Europe. As a consulting
engineer in the 1890s, he defined high standards
of workmanship and on-site supervision. By
1900 contractors worked on his behalf in most
European countries on buildings of many kinds,
some 17,692 contracts having been completed
by 1917.

Louis Gustave Mouchel, the agent for the Hennebique system in Britain, was the French consul in South Wales. His first major project was Weaver's Flour Mill, Swansea, built in 1897–8, and designed by Hennebique in collaboration with Napoleon le Brun. In the following decade Mouchel fulfilled some 600 contracts in Britain, including water tanks, granaries, locomotive depots, office blocks, grain silos and quays. The Hennebique system proved to have particular merits for warehouses and granaries. The Co-operative Wholesale Society warehouse on the quayside at Newcastle upon Tyne is probably the oldest surviving major ferro-concrete building in England (58). It was built in 1897–1900, the design being developed by F. E. L. Harris of the CWS, and T. G. Guerrite, an engineer with Mouchel's firm. A thick raft, almost 2m (6½ft)

58 The Co-operative Wholesale Society Warehouse on the quayside at Newcastle upon Tyne, built in 1897–1900 to the design of F. E. L. Harris of the CWS and the firm of L. G. Mouchel. (Michael Stratton)

deep, supported the seven-storey building. Its columns, floors and roof were all constructed of concrete. The CWS subsequently erected ferro-concrete structures in their complex at Dunston, where a soapworks, later converted to a hide-and-skin works, was given a Renaissance appearance by the society's architect, L. G. Ekins (59).

These French firms had every incentive to keep their patented systems shrouded in mystery. One English engineer, Oscar Faber, did much to help entrepreneurs and designers unravel this confusing world of aggregate mixes, bar angles and shuttering details. Faber gained a broad working knowledge of concrete through fabricating wharves, jetties and chimneys for Associated Portland Cement Manufacturers Ltd. He transferred to the Indented Bar Co. in time to work on buildings for the Gramophone Co. works at Hayes (now EMI Records). This experience enabled him to produce the first British practical manual on concrete construction in 1912.

Americans shared this down-to-earth approach to concrete. Julius Kahn, a member of a Detroit family of architect and engineers, patented a simple but effective reinforcing bar in 1903, and established the Trussed Concrete Steel Co., later Truscon, to make and market it (see 57). The European branch of Truscon, founded in 1907 by his brother, Moritz Kahn promoted the system in Britain (60). It was closely associated with the multi-storey daylight factory, and with the stylish factories designed by Wallis, Gilbert & Partners (see Chapter 8).

The employment of concrete was stimulated by government restrictions on the use of steel during World War I and the need for protection against fire and explosion in armaments works. In the 1920s the balance shifted again. Steel was available in stock sizes, allowing clear roof spans from 7.6m (25ft) to well over 30m (98ft). Meanwhile problems remained with the use of concrete, with its requirements for expensive mixing plant and care in the erection of shuttering (the wooden boarding which holds concrete in place while it sets). Prejudice continued against

59 A Co-operative Wholesale Society factory at Dunston-on-Tyne, a concrete building in the Renaissance style, regarded by the society as 'unusually attractive'. It was designed by L. G. Ekins, and opened on 15 February 1909. It was later used as a hide-and-skin works. (Michael Stratton)

60 A surviving portion of one of three blocks, 183m (600ft) long, built from 1914 for the Birmingham Small Arms Co. (BSA), Small Heath, Birmingham. The structure was designed with a concrete frame on the Kahn system by the Trussed Concrete Steel Co. Ltd (Truscon). (Michael Stratton)

systems developed by foreigners, and available only through licensed contractors.

For two centuries, the acceptance of iron, steel and concrete had lagged behind the work of pioneering industrialists and their designers. Perhaps the most significant aspects of this drawn-out saga, apart from the transition to a full internal frame and non-structural walls, are the increasingly close collaborations established between engineer and architect in the design of factories. Within this broad context the desirability of rapid erection, easy access and adaptability came to outweigh concerns over fireproofing and natural lighting, as electricity became the prime source of light and power in the inter-war period.

6
Making machines

Shaping iron was one of the characteristic activities of the Industrial Revolution. Just as coal was the essential fuel of the period, so iron was its archetypal material.

During the Industrial Revolution the British learned how to make machines of iron. This was one of the most significant changes of the period, yet it is one of the least well defined. The purpose of this chapter is to show how machine-building became a distinctive aspect of manufacturing, how it has maintained an essential continuity over the past two centuries, and how the industry's surviving buildings illuminate its past.

There were few machines in the eighteenth century. Clocks and similar instruments were made of small pieces of precision-worked metal. Larger less intricate machines were made by millwrights. The whole of a watermill could be regarded as a machine: the foundations, the walls of the building, the taking-in doors, as well as the waterwheel, the shafts, the gearing, the stones in their tuns and the hoist. The same could be said of a windmill, a fulling mill or a horse-driven hoist at a mine. To construct such a machine involved the labour of bricklayers or stonemasons and carpenters, as well as millwrights who provided gearing and shafting.

Steam engines and water frames

The steam engine, the most important machine invented and developed in the eighteenth century, fits into this tradition. Many textbooks describe how Boulton & Watt sold steam engines to entrepreneurs. They would assess the customer's requirements, produce drawings, fabricate the valves, and provide an erector, but it was the customer who had to purchase the wood, the bricks and the iron castings and forgings which made up the greater part of the engine. The only novel feature of the process was that a performance indicator was fitted to the engine, and Boulton & Watt received a royalty calculated on the basis of what the customer saved by using one of their engines instead of the earlier type of Newcomen engine. Other aspects of the process were commonplace. Most steam engines were purchased in this way. While the role of Boulton & Watt as designers might be taken by an ironfounder, what he supplied was a set of parts for the customer to erect, not a working machine. The Newcomen engine at Elsecar near Sheffield was erected in 1794–5 in this way.

The water frame for spinning cotton, the invention of Richard Arkwright, which was first used in a water-powered factory at Cromford in 1771, is an archetypal machine of a different kind. A machine from Cromford which probably dates from Arkwright's time is preserved at the Helmshore Textile Museum. It is of wooden construction. Power was conveyed to it by leather belts attached to shafting in the mill, which ran around wooden drums. The intricate components, including the fluted rollers which were essential to its success, look like parts of a clock, and Arkwright had indeed sought the skills of clockmakers when he was manufacturing his machines. The need for such expertise highlights another aspect of the development of engineering. It was necessary not only to be able to make castings and forgings, but to shape them with precision. The machine shop was an essential part of the evolving engineering works.

Machining munitions

The emergence of the company which could design, manufacture and install a machine was a significant feature of the Industrial Revolution. The first such companies were ironworking concerns which supplied cannon to the army and navy. Excavations in the Weald have shown that cannon were cast in the eighteenth century at several of the region's water-powered blast furnaces. Molten iron from the furnace was released to run along a channel made in sand, covering the floor, to moulds set vertically on tables in timber-lined and well-drained pits. Castings for cannon had to be bored to a precise internal diameter. There were several water-powered boring mills in the Weald. Excavations at Pippingford revealed the base of a boring machine, together with the four cast-iron wheels of the trolley on which guns had been mounted while being bored. A wrought-iron boring bar, 3.35m (11ft) long, with three of its four cutters in place in the head, was found in the early 1970s at Stream Furnace, Chiddingly, and is preserved at the Anne of Cleves Museum at Lewes.

The Wealden ironworks used charcoal as their fuel, and their fortunes declined in the course of the eighteenth century. The manufacture of castings became the concern of ironworks where blast furnaces were fired with coke rather than charcoal, a process first used successfully by Abraham Darby at Coalbrookdale in 1709. Darby and his successors developed a trade in domestic utensils, together with some railings and columns for porches. Such ironworks also made

parts for machines, stamps for crushing ore in Cornish mines, wheels for railway wagons and, above all, cylinders and pipes for steam engines.

The first foundries

A distinct change can be observed during the 1790s. In part this was due to developments in the technology of the steam engine and of other machines, and in part to the gradual spread of foundry techniques.

Many engineers were endeavouring to improve the steam engine, among them Richard Trevithick, pioneer of high-pressure steam. He, with others, designed engines which could be free-standing, of which walls and foundations were not integral parts. The Trevithick engine displayed in the Science Museum, London, is an example. At the same time other engineers were designing machines to be worked by steam engines, to spin or weave fabrics, to manufacture paper or to crush sugar-cane. Most such machines incorporated iron castings.

Specialist foundries making engineering castings were a new phenomenon in the 1790s. The best known was the Soho Foundry in Smethwick, opened by Boulton & Watt in 1796. Boulton & Watt had previously not supplied engine parts, except for valves, but the impending expiry of Watt's patents in 1800 led them to establish a works where they could make complete machines. In 1795, in Leeds, Matthew Murray, the engineer who was responsible for the machines which transformed flax manufacturing, set up with partners the company of Murray, Fenton & Wood of the Round Foundry. They made flax machinery, iron frames for flax mills, steam engines and, from 1812, locomotives for the nearby Middleton Railway. The foundry took its name from its principal building, a circular assembly shop. This has been demolished, but most of the other buildings remain.

The first specialist engineering works in Manchester were established in the 1790s. A sale notice of 1810 for a small foundry in the city identifies the components of an engineering works of this period. The buildings were arranged in a quadrangle. The two-storey foundry building measured 69 by 23m (226 by 75½ft), and contained air furnaces as well as cupolas, and cranes 'of extraordinary power'. There were patternmakers' and turners' shops, and a boring mill. The machinery was worked by an 18hp engine which also provided blast for the cupolas.

Market-town foundries

By the time of the Great Exhibition of 1851 factories which could make machines had been established in most significant market towns in England by millwrights, ironmongers and blacksmiths. Castings were made for use in buildings, for watermills, for threshing machines, and for an increasing variety of farm implements.

The Great Exhibition of 1851 provided opportunities for the foundry businesses which had grown up in the previous half-century to display their wares. The catalogues mention machines assembled from castings, forgings and wood in market towns of modest size. William Crosskill from Beverley displayed a steam engine, W. & J. Rodenhurst of Market Drayton a cheese-press, Joseph Grant of Stamford a chaff machine.

The spread by 1851 of engineering techniques to every town of consequence in England depended upon improvements in transport. Coastal shipping, inland navigation and the railways created a national market for the foundryman's principal materials: pig-iron and coke. In 1849 a founder at Plymouth was using Scottish iron or Welsh iron from Clydach, and a foundry in Hornchurch mixed scrap with pig-iron from the Old Park Co. in Shropshire.

Some engineering firms of modest size specialized in products for national markets. In Leamington, Sidney Flavel's Eagle Foundry and other works made household ranges, usually called 'kitcheners'. Stothert & Pitt of Bath developed a local foundry business into a crane-manufacturing concern which supplied world markets. Some specialisms originated in local

demands. In Reading the Katesgrove Works of Barrett, Exall and Andrews made many agricultural machines, but specialized in machinery for baking biscuits, responding to demands from their neighbours Huntley & Palmer, biscuit manufacturers.

Casting from cupolas

The proliferation of foundries depended on various technological factors. Most castings in the eighteenth century had been made at blast furnaces. When a furnace was tapped some of the iron would be drained into a pit, from which it was ladled into mould boxes. Such a method restricted the size of castings. A furnace was normally tapped only twice a day. In 1800 when output could be around 50 tons a week, less than 4 tons could be expected at each tapping. An alternative was the use of an 'air furnace', in which pig-iron or scrap could be remelted before being cast. The earliest known air furnaces were at Coalbrookdale, where two were in existence by 1718. An air furnace is a form of *reverberatory* furnace. It has two 'boxes' separated by a low wall of firebrick or refractory stone. A fire burns in one, while the metal is in the other, in a far corner of which is a flue, which draws heat from the fire across the metal. The only old one to survive in Britain is at the British Ironworks at Abersychan in Gwent.

An alternative to the air furnace was the cupola, a shaft furnace, fired with coke, and blown by several tuyères (pipes carrying air). It was patented by the ironmaster John Wilkinson in 1794 but was generally believed to be the invention of his brother William. Cupolas are now made from sheet steel, lined with refractory bricks, and blown by electric fans. An early example, preserved at Ironbridge, consists of wrought-iron staves, bound together rather like a barrel.

Making machine tools

The cupola made possible the production of iron castings in most towns, but the standard of finishing acceptable for domestic or architectural castings was unsuitable if castings were to be used in machines. The regular production of machines was made possible by the development of machine tools which could finish within precise tolerances both castings and forgings.

The first of significance was the boring mill. During the 1750s the Dutchman Jan Verbruggen developed a means of boring cannon from the solid by feeding a rigid boring bar and cutter horizontally against the casting while it was rotating. His design was copied by John Wilkinson, and modified for finishing engine cylinders, which were of much greater diameter than cannon, and were cast hollow. Wilkinson's machine, which lost its short-lived patent protection in 1779, made possible the Watt steam engine. It was the first of the significant machine tools of the Industrial Revolution. The boring mill house at Coalbrookdale, where a Wilkinson type machine was installed in 1780, remains intact.

Many important developments in machine tools were made in London. The workshop of Henry Maudslay, in Oxford Street between 1798 and 1810, and then in Lambeth, was a nursery of engineering ability. Among those who worked for him were James Nasmyth, inventor of the steam hammer in 1839 (see **62**), Richard Roberts, who was responsible for developments in lathes and planing machines, and Sir Joseph Whitworth, famed for his uniform system of screw threads, first suggested in 1841.

Maudslay made the machines for making wooden pulley blocks in Portsmouth Dockyard. Designed by Sir Marc Brunel, they were perhaps the first machines intended for what would now be called mass production. Maudslay's other products included small steam engines, calico printing equipment, lathes and steam engines for ships. Nasmyth, Roberts and Whitworth also worked in Manchester, and in that city, as in Leeds, the development of ever more complex machines for preparing, spinning and weaving textiles, went hand in hand with the improvement of the machine tools needed to manufacture them. By 1851 the entrepreneur

setting up an engineering works in any town in England could obtain from manufacturers in London, Manchester or Leeds any machine tools which he was likely to need.

The first locomotive builders

A great change came over engineering in the 1830s with the success of the steam railway locomotive. In England, unlike most continental countries, the principal railway companies came to build their own locomotives and carriages. Nevertheless 'private' builders flourished, supplying the large companies when their own production facilities proved inadequate, selling locomotives to the smaller companies which lacked the capacity to build their own, supplying industrial concerns with shunting locomotives, and exporting.

An engineering works which has links with some important early locomotives is the New Foundry in Bradley Road, Stourbridge, part of an ironworks established in 1800 by John Bradley, and described in 1821 as 'the largest & most complete of any in this part of the country & perhaps the most so of any in England' (**61**). In 1819 Bradley's successor, James Foster, formed a nominally separate company in partnership with the engineer John Urpeth Rastrick. The following year Rastrick began surveying for the New Foundry building, which measures 60 by 15m (197 by 49ft). It has an iron roof with wrought-iron rafters and massive cast-iron tie beams; in the centre of each is a cast boss designed to accommodate the top of a pillar crane. It was in this building that two celebrated locomotives were built under Rastrick's direction. *Agenoria*, constructed for the Pensnett Railway in 1828, is displayed in the National Railway Museum at York, and *Stourbridge Lion*, the first locomotive to run on rails in the United States, is exhibited at the Smithsonian Institution in Washington DC.

One of the best-planned engineering works of the 1830s was the Bridgewater Foundry at Patricroft established by James Nasmyth in 1836–8. Nasmyth had previously built steam

61 An early twentieth-century view of the New Foundry, Bradley Road, Stourbridge, showing one of the cast-iron pillar cranes which rotate from bosses in the tie beams of the trusses that support the roof. (Collection: Dr Paul Collins)

engines and machine tools on the first floor of a tenemented cotton mill in central Manchester (**62**). He moved because the vibration of his machine tools threatened the stability of the building, and on one occasion an engine beam crashed through the floor into the shop of a glassworker. Nasmyth built his new works on an open site alongside the Bridgewater Canal and the Liverpool and Manchester Railway, where there was clay for brickmaking on top of sandstone which provided solid foundations for heavy structures.

The first works built specifically to construct locomotives was established in Forth Street, Newcastle upon Tyne, as early as 1823 by George Stephenson and managed by his son Robert (**63, 64**). The locomotive works is set on the western side of South Street, off Forth Street, and squeezed between Newcastle Central station and the River Tyne. Apart from the office block, there are two key surviving sections. The boiler manufactory is of piered brick construction, six bays long and three bays wide. The interior is subdivided by two lines of cast-iron columns, with simple arched bracing, and supporting heavy queen-post wooden trusses. At the western extremity of the site, an area now occupied by a building supplies firm, one bay width survives of what is believed to have been a locomotive erecting shop. Like much else of the complex, the walls are of brick and were pierced with narrow round-headed windows. Cast-iron columns and even wooden columns support heavy wooden beams in places in the form of a crude lattice. The works was extended several times in the nineteenth century.

XX J.Nº FLAT.
O GLASS CUTTER
R. WREN & BENNET MY LANDLORDS
Z MY SMITHY IN THE CELLAR.

MY FACTORY FLAT AT MANCHESTER.

62 A textile mill in Manchester which by the 1830s had been tenemented and was used by tenants for a variety of industrial purposes. James Nasmyth built steam engines in the bays marked X on the second floor, and had a small smithy in the cellar marked Z. (Ironbridge Gorge Museum Trust)

The Great Western Railway decided in 1840 to establish a locomotive works at Swindon alongside its line from Bristol to London (**65**). The first buildings were a running shed 150m (492ft) long, parallel to the main line, with four through tracks. It was ornamented by stone plaques of a *Firefly* class locomotive, which now adorn the office building occupied by the Royal Commission on the Historical Monuments of England. At right angles to the running shed was a 135m (443ft) long and 43m (141ft) wide repair shop, famously illustrated by the artist John Cook Bourne. The shop consisted of three parallel ranges, the outer ones with conventional timber roofs, and the central bay with composite trusses of wrought iron and timber.

63 Exterior of the administration block of Robert Stephenson's locomotive factory of the 1820s, now nos. 18–20 South Street, Newcastle upon Tyne. (RCHME)

64 The interior of Robert Stephenson's locomotive factory of the 1820s at Newcastle upon Tyne. It is supposed that this part of the works was used as a locomotive erecting shop. (Michael Stratton)

65 The Great Western Railway locomotive works at Swindon of the 1840s. The two-storey building was the machine shop of the original works, which was powered by a steam engine housed in two bays within the two lower storeys of the four-storey block to the right, which is an office block of 1926, constructed around and incorporating the older building. (Michael Stratton)

The outer ranges were divided into twenty bays, each capable of accommodating two locomotives, while in the central bay was a traverser, by which locomotives were moved to and from the repair bays. The west wall of the shop survives and forms the boundary of a car-park. Many of the buildings which comprised the locomotive works of the 1840s still stand. The original erecting shop was a relatively small building at right angles to the repair shop, at its north-eastern corner. It accommodated only eighteen locomotives but was equipped with a timber and wrought-iron overhead crane. Grouped around these buildings were smiths' shops, a steam hammer shop, a turning shop equipped with Whitworth lathes, a gigantic slotting machine and a boring machine, a foundry and a copperworking shop. The outline of the steam engine house which provided power for these shops is visible in the wall of the four-storey, eleven-bay office block, erected in 1926. The components of the works were built to a standardized formula. Masonry was of limestone locally quarried or from the Bath

area. Most of the buildings were of pier-and-panel construction. Pillars or columns were spaced at 11ft 7¼in (3.53m) intervals, the intervening spaces being filled either by timber frames with windows and slatting, or by stone masonry built to sill level, with timber slatting and windows above.

The earliest substantially intact example of the first generation of railway works is the former works of the Midland Railway at Derby (**66**).

Building iron ships

Shipbuilding was another form of engineering which grew rapidly in the mid-nineteenth century. The nursery of the iron-hulled, steam-powered ship in England was the River Thames, whose banks below the Port of London were lined with works such as the Thames Ironworks and John Scott Russell's yard on the Isle of Dogs where I. K. Brunel's colossal SS *Great Eastern* was launched after

66 The interior of the roundhouse at Derby Railway Works, established jointly by the Midland Counties Railway, the North Midland Railway and the Birmingham and Derby Junction Railway in 1839. The roundhouse was designed by Francis Thompson for the North Midland Railway and completed in 1839. It is a sixteen-sided polygon in plan, and is built of brick with a circular colonnade of cast-iron columns supporting a timber roof. (RCHME)

much difficulty in 1858. In principle a shipyard was much like a works making locomotives, reapers or printing machines. Parts were fabricated and finished in workshops, but were assembled in a dry dock or on a slipway rather than in an assembly shop. In England shipbuilding withered away in London in the second half of the nineteenth century while it flourished on Merseyside, Tyneside and Wearside. There are no outstanding monuments of the nineteenth century, and few indeed of the later period of steel-ship construction. The best-preserved British-style foundry and forge buildings used in building merchant ships are probably those of the Neorion Shipyard at Hermoupolis on the Greek island of Siros, set up by a British engineer, David Smith, in the 1860s.

The most important evidence of this phase of shipbuilding in England is a range of buildings in the Portsmouth Naval Dockyard constructed after the propeller-driven HMS *Rattler* was shown to be superior to paddle vessels in 1840. The buildings are grouped around the 2.8ha (7-acre) Steam Basin excavated between 1843 and 1848. The oldest is the Steam or West Factory, a 180m (590ft) long, two-storey structure in the style of Vanbrugh, completed in 1848 and constructed in brick, with Portland stone cornices and pedimented bays. The upper storey was carried in a single span on brick vaulting supported by metal girders, and accommodated shops for millwrights, turners and patternmakers. On the ground floor were a heavy turning shop, an erecting shop, a punching and shearing shop, and a boiler shop. A manually operated gantry crane installed for movement of heavy engine and boiler assemblies remains *in situ*. The Steam Factory and probably the adjacent buildings were designed by Sir William Denison of the Royal Engineers.

Victorian engineering works

An engineering works needed access for coal, coke, iron and timber, often achieved by location on a canal bank. It was also essential to be able to remove finished products, so railway sidings often formed part of a works. Foundries, smiths' hearths and heavy machine tools were usually accommodated in single-storey buildings. Many foundry buildings are distinguished by clerestory louvered ventilators running lengthways along their roofs. Machine shops were usually powered by line-shafting connected to a steam engine, which might also provide power for the fans of cupolas. Many engineering works used considerable quantities

of wood, and most included saw mills powered by the steam engines which drove the machine tools. Some foundries were planned around quadrangles, with wagon arches in the front ranges to allow access for delivery vehicles. A 'break-iron', a tripod on which a heavy weight could be lifted on a pulley and then dropped to smash pieces of scrap, was a frequent ornament of a foundry courtyard.

A billhead illustration of John Howard's foundry at Bedford in the late 1830s shows the essential features of an engineering works (**67**). Two ranges of buildings stand at right angles, partially enclosing a yard. From one range protrude the flues from what is obviously a range of smiths' hearths, while a much larger flue in the other building is likely to be from the cupola, and the chimney served the boilers that powered the steam engine. The billheading makes clear the origins of this particular works in Howard's ironmonger's shop. By 1861 Howard was employing 450 men in his Britannia Foundry, a name which was shared with works in Banbury, Derby, Manchester, Oswestry, Market Drayton, Nottingham and Gainsborough.

By the 1840s the focus of most large engineering works was an erecting shop – a high building divided into bays for the assembly of new machines, or disassembly prior to the repair of existing ones, with an overhead crane, capable of lifting traction engines or locomotives. Gantry cranes had their origins in quarries and on civil-engineering sites. Sir John Rennie in 1816 had designed cranes of this type for the West India Docks where they were used for lifting imported mahogany. The concept may have been taken from the docks by Thameside shipbuilders, and from them spread to locomotive works. In 1837 Robert Stephenson & Co. in Newcastle were still using shear legs to lift large components of locomotives, but in the early 1840s the erecting shop and boiler shop at the Great Western Railway works at Swindon were designed to accommodate overhead cranes. Five overhead cranes in the Railway Foundry at Leeds were probably installed when E. B. Wilson

67 A bill issued in 1838 by John Howard of Bedford, ironmonger and owner of the Britannia Foundry, showing his shop and his works. The four flues along the south range indicate the position of the smiths' shop. The wide central flue is probably from the cupola furnace. The tall chimney is probably from the boilers which supplied the steam engine working the machine tools and the cupola fan. The patterns and other items in the yard illustrate the similarities between factories and farmyards discussed in Chapter 3. (Bodleian Library, John Johnson: Bill Headings, Box 15)

reorganized the works in 1848, and Richard Peacock installed similar cranes in the Manchester, Sheffield and Lincolnshire Railway works at Gorton, Manchester, in 1846–8, and in the adjacent works which he set up with Charles Frederick Beyer in 1854. In that year Joseph Glynn remarked, in *The Construction of Cranes and Machinery*, that:

In designing new buildings for steam engine manufacturers the side walls are now generally made of sufficient strength to carry a line of rails upon an offset of masonry. In these rails rest two parallel frames of timber mounted on low wheels at each end ... so that the frames may travel along the building ... upon these frames a carriage travels similar to those in the mahogany shed.

The outstanding monument of the market-town foundries of the mid-nineteenth century is the Long Shop, sometimes called the 'cathedral' – the erecting shop of the works of Richard Garrett at Leiston in Suffolk (**colour plate 9**). The firm originated in 1778 but only began to make castings on a large scale in the 1830s. After the completion of the Long Shop in 1853 the company achieved fame as a maker of

traction engines. The firm employed over 800 men by 1861. The Long Shop is a tall, brick-built structure with iron-framed windows. It has a queen-post roof, with cast-iron trusses bearing the inscription 'RG [Richard Garrett] 1853' linking timber uprights. A timber gallery runs round the building at first-floor level, and there are traces of line-shafting in the aisles beneath. The building is now a museum.

Agricultural machines

Growth in the engineering industry accelerated after the Great Exhibition of 1851. For small towns, a foundry became a matter of prestige. A meeting of the inhabitants of Buckingham in 1855 decided that the town's economy needed a foundry, and resolved to form the Buckingham Castle Ironworks Co. It did not succeed, but many engineers making agricultural machines in towns no bigger than Buckingham served international markets. In Norfolk alone more than thirty firms manufactured steam engines in the second half of the nineteenth century (68).

One of the most significant exhibits at the Great Exhibition was the McCormick reaper, the invention of a farmer's son from Virginia, which was rated by the Berkshire agriculturist

68 The Tuscan-style lettering, doubtless cast within the building, which announces the identity of Thomas Smithdale's foundry at Panxworth, Norfolk, built in 1869. (Michael Stratton)

Philip Pusey with the spinning-jenny and the power loom. A licence to build the machine in Britain was obtained by Bernhard Samuelson of Banbury. The reaper and the more complex haymaking and binder machines which evolved from it demanded new modes of production. Samuelson and other agricultural engineers moved towards what became known as the American System of Manufactures. They produced large numbers of identical or near-identical machines, with interchangeable parts, assembling them in erecting shops from machined castings and forgings, and from wooden parts made elsewhere on the site.

Later locomotive works

Locomotive building continued to expand in the second half of the nineteenth century. Existing private builders like Beyer Peacock of Manchester looked increasingly to distant colonial markets as competition from German firms increased on the European mainland, while new companies like Fox Walker of Bristol established in 1864, W. G. Bagnall of Stafford established in 1875, and Hunslet in Leeds which dates from 1863, specialized in industrial shunting locomotives.

The National Railway Museum has calculated that some 109,000 steam locomotives were built in Britain between 1800 and 1960, divided among the principal locomotive engineering towns, as shown in table 2.

Table 2:

Numbers of locomotives built in
British towns, 1800–1960

Glasgow	26,000
Manchester	20,500
Leeds	12,100
Tyneside	9,500
Crewe	7,300
Swindon	6,000
Bristol	4,200
Darlington	4,000
Derby	3,000
London	2,700
Kilmarnock	2,500
Doncaster	2,200
Horwich	1,800
Stoke-on-Trent	1,700
Stafford	1,700
Brighton	1,200
Sheffield	800
Wolverhampton	800
Ashford	800
Eastleigh	300
Inverness	40
Total	109,140

Source: National Railway Museum

The main railway companies extended their works. At Swindon the works was extended in the 1870s, and in June 1900 directors of the Great Western company authorized the construction of the first part of what became known as 'A' Shop (**69**). This was a vast machining and erecting shop, measuring 146 by 148m (479 by 485½ft) and covering some 2.12ha (5 acres). It was the first building at Swindon where the framework was entirely of steel, and set the pattern for numerous subsequent twentieth-century engineering works. The walls were of smooth-faced red bricks, with blue engineering brick. All the machinery was electrically powered. 'A' Shop was doubled in size in 1919, and between 1923 and 1950 the 'Castle' and 'King' class locomotives were constructed there. While substantial parts remain of the nineteenth-century works at Swindon, 'A' Shop has been demolished.

The most substantial new works of the late nineteenth century was built at Horwich near Bolton between 1884 and 1887 by the Lancashire and Yorkshire Railway, who moved there from a congested site at Newton Heath, Manchester (**colour plate 10**). The works employed 3000 men by 1894, and continued to build locomotives until the 1960s. It has been adapted as an industrial estate and most of the buildings remain – lengthy, high-roofed, single-storey sheds with their roofs carried on cast-iron columns. The walls are in local brick, with projecting piers and deep, metal-framed windows. Horwich incorporated the most advanced thinking of the 1880s. It was planned to allow materials to progress through the works with a minimum of 'doubling-back'. The foundry and forge were close to the pattern shop and wheel-turning department, and to the machining and boiler shops. These in turn were adjacent to the erecting shop, which had accommodation for 90 engines and 30 tenders and was equipped with electric traversers. The works yard was planned with sidings for locomotives, a wagon weighing-machine, space for stacks of timber, coal, coke, pig-iron, wrought-iron and cast-iron scrap, and for tipping ashes, a reservoir and a filtration plant for recovered water.

Mechanical and electrical engineers

Most general heavy engineering works of the late nineteenth century were situated in

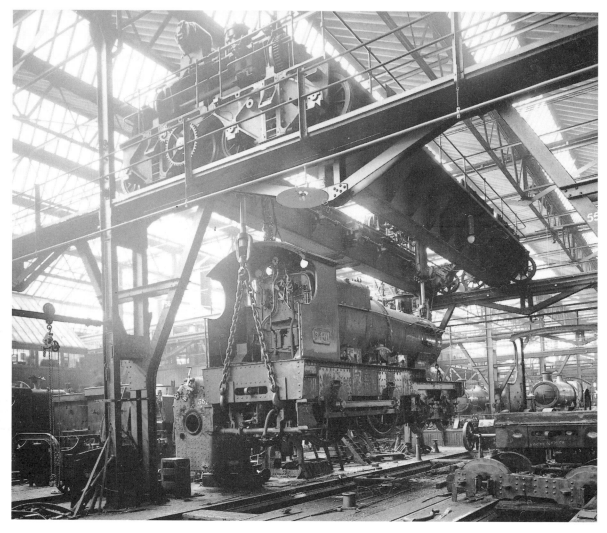

69 'A' Shop at the Great Western Railway's locomotive works at Swindon, construction of which commenced in 1900. The area of the shop was doubled in 1919, and it was used for the construction of the company's main-line locomotives until 1950. (Swindon Railway Museum)

coalfields or in big cities, unlike those making agricultural implements or locomotives, which were to be found in many towns of modest size. The New Yard at St George's, Telford, was established by the Lilleshall Company, previously a mining and ironmaking concern, in 1861, and became one of England's principal engineering firms (**70**). By the early 1870s there were more than seventy machine tools in the machine shop, two steam hammers in the forge,

and cranes in the foundry capable of lifting the heaviest castings then in demand. At the turn of the century steam pumping engines were supplied for the waterworks in Shanghai, and a large gas engine for a railway company in Japan. The works closed in 1931 but remains in use as tenemented industrial units. Its arcaded frontage has been little altered. Elsewhere in Telford, the 77m (253ft) long, 12m (39ft) wide erecting shop of the Coalbrookdale works, built in 1878–9 when the company was expanding its engineering activities, now forms part of the Ironbridge Gorge Museum (**71**).

The dominant engineering works in the north-east was the Elswick plant set up on the western side of Newcastle upon Tyne in 1847 by Sir William Armstrong, initially to produce hydraulic machinery, although by 1900 it was used principally for the production of armaments.

From the 1880s engineers were increasingly interested in electricity, both as a source of lighting and as a means of transmitting power, and some realized that high-speed engines were well suited to power generators. Among them were Peter Willans and Mark Robinson, who occupied a constricted site at Thames Ditton, Surrey. In 1894 they decided to move to Rugby, where their substantial factory was completed in 1897. The new works, designed by T. W. Willard, was from the start planned on a grand scale on a 9.3ha (23-acre) site, and by 1900 employed 950 people. Components progressed

by a flow system from the foundry to the machine shop, then to the erecting shop and packing area. All the production buildings were high, single-storey north-lit sheds, of lattice steel construction. By 1904 the company had turned to the manufacture of steam turbines. Willans & Robinson demanded high standards of accuracy and followed an enlightened labour policy, expressed not least in the quality of their

70 Pumping engines for a waterworks in Shanghai under construction in 1927 in the erection shop of the Lilleshall Company's engineering works, the New Yard at St George's, Telford. The works was constructed *c.* 1860, and closed in 1931, although the buildings remain as tenemented industrial units. (Ironbridge Gorge Museum Trust)

building, which was intended to match the architectural standards set by William Butterfield in his extensions to Rugby School.

The most dramatic development in electric engineering in Britain was the construction in 1901–3 by the American pioneer of electrification, George Westinghouse, of a huge factory on the industrial estate at Trafford Park, Manchester (72). Unlike most British engineering concerns which grew from small beginnings, the Westinghouse works was enormous from the start. Westinghouse anticipated that the main-line railways in

Europe would be electrified, and established a factory to supply their equipment. The main machine shop was 274m (899ft) long and 134m (440ft) wide, with three aisles, and followed a pattern of clerestory construction which can be observed in many North American engineering works. For nearly a century the Trafford Park works was the most important engineering concern in Britain, producing steam turbines, generators, electric motors of all kinds, radar equipment and, during World War II, Lancaster bombers.

The traditional engineering works which evolved in mid-Victorian England, with foundries and forges clustered around an assembly shop, has been used in the twentieth century principally for the production of heavy machines in small batches, for locomotives, electricity-generating plant and large machine tools. Such factories have proved versatile. Most

71 The engineering shop of 1878–9 at the Coalbrookdale works in the Ironbridge Gorge, showing the overhead crane, with blacksmiths working at their hearths, machine tools driven by belts from shafting, and engines under construction, all in the same building. (Ironbridge Gorge Museum Trust)

locomotive works were adapted to produce armaments in both world wars for example. Nevertheless such works have tended to be overshadowed by the motor-car and aircraft plants considered in Chapter 3, which are largely derived from different traditions.

72 One of the steel-framed shops in George Westinghouse's engineering works at Trafford Park, Manchester, shortly before production commenced in 1903, showing machine tools being delivered by train on the last stage of their journey from the United States via the Manchester Ship Canal. (Ironbridge Gorge Museum Trust)

7

More than safe storage: the warehouse

Warehouses were among the architectural show-pieces of the Industrial Revolution. Huge brick-and-stone-walled structures, often over four-storeys high, still flank harbour fronts, canals and railways and dominate the centres of the great textile cities.

The role of the warehouse extended beyond the protection of goods from the weather and thieving hands. A warehouse might be a place where dutiable imported goods were kept in bond until it suited an importer to pay customs duty. It might be where a wholesaler displayed his stock. The term might be used to describe a retailing establishment where such ready-made goods as footwear or furniture were offered for sale. A manufacturer's warehouse might be part of a factory where products, raw materials, components or part-made goods were stored. Most Victorian and Edwardian textile warehouses were located in city centres, at some distance from mills or dyehouses but ideally located to act as showrooms and points of dispatch by railway. Although different in form, a modern storage installation, a cluster of grain silos or oil-storage tanks may be part of a productive unit, a corn mill or an oil refinery, or, alternatively, a remote, self-contained enterprise located at a transport interchange and used only for storage.

The seasonal nature of the harvest and the unpredictability of global trade by sailing-ship dictated the need for secure storage long before the Industrial Revolution. The tithe barn is the most impressive medieval precursor of the industrial warehouse, having a vast interior approached through a central entrance high enough for a loaded wagon. The largest conserved wooden barns are at Coggeshall and Cressing Temple in Essex, while there is a fine fourteenth-century stone example at Bradford-on-Avon in Wiltshire.

Coastal precedents

Merchants involved in overseas trade invested in impressive warehouses as early as the fifteenth century. Such warehouses might be set between their houses and wharves as at Kings Lynn, Norfolk, where one timber-framed range, the Hanse Warehouse in St Margaret's Lane, was used for over three centuries from 1428, originally by merchants of the Hanseatic League, an association of merchant guilds from cities in the Rhineland and the Baltic. Storage facilities might be collaboratively funded as a municipal asset. The once busy port of Exeter retains a warehouse built c. 1680, which is now an interpretation centre (73). It rests on the stone footings of an Elizabethan building and on the remains of a wharf of wattle construction probably dating from the medieval period. The new stone and timber warehouse was built to handle imported raw materials and the export of woollen cloth dried on nearby tenterfields. A cantilevered roof protected boats and cargoes, but storage space within the two-storey building was very restricted.

The Royal Navy erected large storehouses from the late seventeenth century to ensure that supplies were available in the event of war. The oldest surviving dockyard storehouse is the clock-tower building at Chatham built in 1723. The most urbane group, comprising nos. 9, 10 and 11 stores at Portsmouth, was built between 1764 and 1784, and is arranged in a long line, whose sense of order is reinforced by arcaded ground floors and central pediments on each block. Such stores were built with internal structures of wood. Fireproof construction was adopted in the nineteenth century for the Quadrangle Storehouse at Sheerness, Kent, designed by Edward Holl in 1822 but now demolished. Cast-iron columns and wrought-iron beams supported floors of York stone.

London docks

Huge brick warehouses were built at coastal and canal ports from the late eighteenth century. Their constructional form is comparable to that

73 The Crane Cellars (now the Quay House visitor centre) on the Quay at Exeter. The building, a form of transit shed, was erected during a substantial programme of port improvement about 1680. (Michael Stratton)

of many contemporary textile mills. Both types of building needed strong floors and a degree of protection against fire. Investment in dock warehousing was justified by new customs measures. As long as duties had to be paid as soon as goods arrived at a port there was every incentive to sell them quickly without waiting to gauge the state of the market. Charters granted in 1661 and 1708 to the East India Company, which handled Britain's trade with Asia, granted the privilege of holding goods in bond – deferring payment of import duty until they were ready for dispatch. During the eighteenth century other merchants gained this privilege on shipments of tobacco, rum, sugar and coffee.

The East India Company built London's first great warehouse complex in Cutler Street in the

City (**74**). The earliest portion is the original four-storey wing of the Old Bengal Warehouse, dating from 1769–70. This block and the adjoining ranges of the 1790s introduce the blunt, symmetrical layout and style, and the constructional features that were to characterize dock architecture well into the next century. The walls are of stock brick; inside timber columns support timber beams and joists, while the staircases are of stone. Bays containing windows are separated by bays with taking-in doors on each storey and projecting hoists above.

A rule imposed by Customs and Excise that goods could only be unloaded at Legal Quays close to the Custom House was relaxed in 1789 and repealed by an Act of Parliament of 1803, making possible the erection of wet docks lined by warehouses downstream from the Pool of London. The first, of which some fragments survive near Canary Wharf, were the warehouses at West India Docks built in 1802–3 (**75**). They

74 The north ends of blocks H, G and D in the Cutler Street warehouse complex in the City of London, built by the East India Company in the late eighteenth century, part of which was converted to offices and apartments in the 1970s. (RCHME)

75 A view of the Isle of Dogs from a panoramic view of London of the early nineteenth century. Beyond the canal constructed by Sir John Rennie across the isthmus of the 'island' *c.* 1800 are the wet docks and warehouses of the West India Docks complex. (Ironbridge Gorge Museum: Elton Collection)

76 To the right of this view can be seen bifurcating cast-iron columns supporting the roof of the New Tobacco Warehouse of 1811–14 in London Docks. For much of its life this building was used not for tobacco but for the import of hides from Australia, and was commonly called the Skin Floor. The building was adapted as a retailing and leisure centre in the 1980s. (RCHME)

were designed by the engineer William Jessop, with stone string courses and cornices and semicircular windows adding an element of Classical grandeur to five- and six-storey blocks.

The design of dock warehouses was influenced by concerns over pilferage and fire. They might be surrounded by high walls, or the warehouses themselves might serve as the outer walls of dock complexes, their outer façades having only a few, small, high-set windows covered with iron grilles. Cast-iron columns and windows and internal firewalls might be incorporated in the design to reduce the fire risk (**76**). Full 'fireproof' construction, with cast-iron beams and brick jack arches, could rarely be justified, since fire hazards were less than in textile mills.

Jesse Hartley at Liverpool

In Liverpool growth in transatlantic and African trade underwrote the creation of numerous wet docks. The Goree Warehouses reconstructed between 1802 and 1810 introduced the form of an open arcaded ground floor to aid cargo handling, while the Duke's Dock Warehouse of 1811 was the first in the port to make structural use of cast iron. Jesse Hartley, newly appointed as surveyor for Liverpool's docks, combined these precedents with ideas drawn from Telford's work in London, in Albert Dock, his first commission as surveyor for the port, executed in 1841–5. The brick façades of the five-storey warehouses are almost flush with the granite dock walls. Each range is set on a ground-floor arcade, originally entirely open, to facilitate the handling of sacks and barrels. Elliptical arches, supported by massive Doric cast-iron columns, gave space for cranes and, with the taking-in doors set above, gave a rhythm to the long, otherwise bland elevations lining all four sides of the near-square dock basin. Hartley adopted forms of structural

77 The two large early nineteenth-century warehouses on the Quay at Exeter. In 1946 Sir Thomas Sharp, the great planner, commended their 'fine sturdy character', and remarked that 'it is no exaggeration to say that these warehouses are among the finest buildings in England. Special steps should be taken to ensure that they are not ignorantly destroyed.' (Michael Stratton)

ironwork used several decades earlier in textile mills. Iron beams of inverted 'Y' or 'V' section support brick arches and tiled floors, even the basement having a vaulted structure. Wrought-iron rods act as stabilizing ties. Even the roof is ferrous, sheets of galvanized iron being riveted to wrought-iron supports. Hartley gave meticulous attention to detail, specially shaped iron sheets set over the stair-wells serving as both roofing and water cisterns for the flush closets. Albert Dock was equipped with twenty-one internal hoists. The narrow sections of warehousing were used as transit sheds, from

which goods – typically imported tea, silk, rice, hemp, cotton, sugar and tobacco – might be moved to different parts of the complex or loaded on to carts. Once unloaded, vessels transferred to the neighbouring Salthouse Dock for loading.

Victorian and Edwardian ports

The form of the dock warehouse became more diversified during the Victorian period (**77**). The growth of food imports and the introduction of new technologies for handling bulk goods resulted in the erection of specialist grain and meat stores. While Wait & James' Bristol Granary of 1869 was designed round a series of sack hoists, the massive Waterloo Dock corn warehouse at Liverpool, completed in the same year, was equipped with elevators for handling imports of grain from the North American prairies. G. F. Lister set five storeys of warehouse above an open colonnade of stone piers, the headgears for the elevators extending up a further two floors as miniature campaniles. Sir W. G. Armstrong & Co. supplied a hydraulic system whereby an accumulator provided the pressure for Archimedean screw pumps and powered conveyor belts. Grain was initially lifted by a 17cwt-capacity hopper which discharged at the top of the building. Ladder elevators and suction tubes were subsequently introduced. By the inter-war period concrete silos, and suction intakes that could lift wheat straight out of a ship into store, had transformed the form and operation of the dockside granary. The best-surviving examples in England are at Avonmouth, Birkenhead (78) and Newcastle upon Tyne.

Traditional warehouses continued to be built into the twentieth century for the storage of tobacco. They were designed to accommodate large barrels called hogsheads and to allow for bundles of leaves to be removed and inspected. Cranes, essential for lifting the hogsheads, would be fixed to the building frame, which would typically be executed in a firepoof

material – iron, steel or concrete – to reduce the hazard of dry leaves exploding into flame. A specialist bonded tobacco warehouse had been built at King's Dock, Liverpool, as early as 1792–3, and in 1900 the city gained 'the world's largest tobacco warehouse' when a 221m (725ft) long, twelve-storey structure was completed at Stanley Dock. G. F. Lister's design still towers over the northern dockland of Liverpool. Its ground floor is now the location for a Sunday market.

Within a few years W. D. & H. O. Wills transferred their import trade from Liverpool to Bristol, and built three huge tobacco warehouses at the western end of the harbour at Cumberland Basin. All are nine storeys high, almost cubic in outline and faced in red brick above a ground floor of blue engineering brick. The first – 'A' bond dating from 1905–6 – has a hybrid iron and steel frame, while 'B' and 'C' of 1908 and 1919 were built with concrete beams

78 Steel-framed and concrete granaries and mills on the north side of the West Float at Birkenhead. (Barrie Trinder)

reinforced on François Coignet's system (see Chapter 5). Each warehouse was equipped with three electric lifts, two hydraulic presses and electric lighting.

Transit sheds

With the exception of warehouses intended specifically for tobacco and grain, fewer multi-storey structures were built from the mid-nineteenth century. Steam vessels, railways and new patterns of distribution and handling meant that shipments could be timetabled more precisely. Dock companies aimed to handle goods speedily, something best achieved with single- or two-storey transit sheds on the dock sides, flanked by railway lines, a pattern adopted at Poplar Docks, London, from the 1860s. Open-sided sheds might be given walls to augment security. In Liverpool the surviving transit sheds on the southern side of West Princes Dock date from the 1880s but were enclosed around 1904–5. New transit sheds were likely to be built with steel frames and lightweight corrugated cladding. A typical dock landscape of this period can be seen on the south side of Bristol harbour where the Industrial Museum, housed in one of the sheds, operates a steam locomotive on the adjacent dock railway.

Developments in crane technology reinforced the advantages of transit sheds on open quays. The hydraulic crane was patented by Sir William Armstrong in 1846, and was soon employed inside traditional warehouses, jiggers magnifying the stroke of a hydraulic piston so that loads could be lifted through several storeys. Movable hydraulic cranes called 'elephants' or 'devils' could be used to shift bales and barrels around a quay or warehouse floor. The skylines of ports came to be marked by ornate pumping stations and accumulator towers that provided the necessary heads of water. The most dramatic hydraulic tower is the 33m (108ft) high campanile designed by J. W. Wild and erected in 1851 at the entrance to Grimsby Docks. Hydraulic dockside cranes

were introduced from 1864 and widely used from the 1880s.

Contemporary developments in bulk handling further reduced the significance of the multi-storey warehouse. The advantages of loading and unloading coal and grain in bulk were soon applied to other goods. Meat, following precedents set in Chicago, was removed from ships' holds by conveyors which led directly to cold stores. Specialist types of conveyor were developed during the Edwardian period for handling chests of tea. Cargo-handling trucks were an even more significant influence in promoting the advantages of single-storey transit sheds. An electric platform truck was developed in 1920 and a lift or 'elevated' truck was tested in Southampton Docks in 1922. Once the fork-lift truck was in widespread use, warehouses were designed and adapted for goods to be strapped to wooden pallets by metal banding. Palletization in turn was complemented by the introduction of ships designed for 'roll-on/roll-off' cargo handling from the 1950s, their design drawing on wartime experience with tank landing craft. The principles of containerization were developed in the United States in the 1950s. The first container ships worked into the Thames at Tilbury in January 1968. Tilbury, Felixstowe and other container ports now have scarcely a warehouse, containers being transferred from ship to lorry or train by electric crane without any break of bulk, and, in a remarkable reversion to pre-industrial practice, simply being stacked in the open air when immediate dispatch is impracticable.

Canal and railway warehouses

With the development of canal and railway networks warehouses proliferated away from the coast (**79**). The first significant canal-served distribution warehouse was built at the Manchester terminus of what is popularly regarded as Britain's first canal. The Grocers' Warehouse was erected at the eastern end of Castlefields basin in the 1770s. Only the

79 The Clock Warehouse on the Trent and Mersey Canal at Shardlow, Derbyshire, originally a transhipment warehouse, but converted in the nineteenth century to a corn mill, and now a visitor centre. (Barrie Trinder)

foundations now remain, but the nearby Merchants' Warehouse of 1827–8 is intact. Two archways provide access to wharves underneath the buildings, from which goods could be raised to the three upper storeys by a hoist set in the attic.

Railways soon usurped canals as the prime means of carrying food and consumer goods. The Liverpool and Manchester Railway, opened in 1830, invested in warehousing to handle the general merchandise that it expected to carry. A twenty-bay long, three-storey warehouse plus basement was erected at the Manchester terminus in Liverpool Road. It now forms the striking centre-piece of the Museum of Science and Industry in Manchester. The structure follows the precedents set by the nearby canal warehouses of Castlefields. Brick walls topped by a line of gables are given sparse stone dressings, while the internal structure is of timber with the exception of a series of brick firebreak walls and the cast-iron columns set in the basement. Crane winches with contra-wound ropes and, from 1831, steam-power, hoisted goods up from street level and down from the railway line set on an embankment at first-storey level. Rapid growth in shipments, especially of cotton, soon necessitated new warehouses. Two new multi-storey structures and a single-storey transit shed were erected in 1831. The latter shed now forms the museum's power hall.

All railway-freight depots were essentially interchanges between road and rail transport. Some were also interchanges with canals. The London and North Western Railway and the Great Northern built depots where their lines crossed the Regent's Canal in north London. The focus of the Great Northern's yard was the Granary built to designs by Lewis Cubitt in 1850–1. Its layout and form reflect many of the

features seen in harbour and canal warehouses.
Boats ran into the basement and into other
shipping holes set under the flanking transit
sheds, designed to segregate arriving and
departing goods. External hoists and taking-in
doors alternated with bays of crescent-headed
windows to allow sacks and barrels to be loaded
directly on and off road wagons.

The Victorian railway warehouse reached a
zenith in 1896–8 with an investment by the
Great Northern Railway in Manchester, to the
east of Castlefields and the Liverpool Road
station and immediately to the north of Central
station (80). The engineer, W. X. Foxlee,
created a multi-level rail, road and canal
interchange, with, in essence, two separate
goods stations set one over the other and served
by high- and low-level railway yards. Wagons
ran down to the lower level where they could be
shunted by hydraulic capstans or moved from
one floor to another by hydraulic lift. Further
hoists provided a connection with an arm of the

80 The warehouse of the Great Northern Railway in
Deansgate, Manchester, built between 1895 and 1898.
Like other large city-centre railway-freight depots, the
warehouse was a complex interchange between rail, canal
and road transport, the various levels being connected by
inclines with hydraulic haulage. This was one of the
buildings in which the use of steel-framing was pioneered
in Britain. The building measures 81 by 66m (266 by
216ft). It is sustained by steel pillars, which carry riveted-
steel cross-beams the spaces between which are spanned
by brick jack arches. (Michael Stratton)

Bridgewater Canal, which gave a link to the
newly completed Manchester Ship Canal. Road
wagons and, later, lorries were loaded under
cover. A broad ramp gave them access to the
first-storey level.

This enormous warehouse, five storeys high
and 81.4m (267ft) long and 66.1m (217ft) wide,
has a traditional appearance, walls of red and blue
brick being emblazoned with huge letters at
cornice level. The elevation to Deansgate has large

external taking-in doors for the four hydraulic lifts. Only by entering what is now a public car-park is it possible to appreciate the technological significance of the GNR warehouse as a 'marvel in mild steel', one of the first large steel-framed buildings in Britain. Box-girder columns support steel beams and a series of steel cross-girders which carry narrow brick arches and hence concrete floors (see **55**). The aim in adopting steel and concrete was to achieve wide spans with adequate strength, rather than perfect fireproofing – an excursion to the top of the building shows a roof supported by timber trusses. The development included ranges of offices and shops, in Peter Street and Deansgate, which were designed, following negotiations with Manchester Corporation, to screen the marshalling yard.

The manufacturing warehouse

A warehouse within a manufacturing complex might be a purely utilitarian store, but it sometimes became an architecturally ornate icon, which represented the company's public image. Some ironworks invested in ornate warehouses. The Coalbrookdale Company built two contrasting structures around 1840: a Gothic crenellated edifice by the River Severn just upstream of the Iron Bridge, designed by Samuel Cookson in the same style as the company school at nearby Dawley, and the Great Warehouse of 1838 set in the heart of their ironworks, with iron window-frames and sills, whose severe appearance was transformed in 1843, by the addition of a decorative iron clock-tower which symbolized Coalbrookdale's skills in the manufacture of ornamental castings.

Textile manufacturers needed warehouses for a variety of purposes: for holding raw materials, semi-finished products or goods awaiting dispatch, and also for finishing, inspecting and displaying fabrics and made-up garments. Flax mills characteristically have sparsely fenestrated, fireproof warehouses for the storage of bundles of flax, which were imported seasonally from Flanders, the Baltic and Ireland. The flax warehouse at the

Ditherington Flax Mill, Shrewsbury, whose main mill was built in 1796–7, was completed by June 1805 (**81**). A similar warehouse survives at Marshall's Mill, Leeds.

A warehouse within a mill complex was typically aligned at a right angle to the main range. The most impressive factory warehouse must be the five-storey, forty-four-bay range at Manningham Mill, Bradford, built to designs from Andrews & Pepper in 1871–3 (**82**). The structure, built parallel to the spinning mill, was fireproof with iron columns and beams supporting concrete arches. Deep windows provided lighting for sorting raw wool and examining finished cloth. Their Italian Renaissance detailing was echoed in the cornice of the soaring campanile chimney.

81 The windowless, iron-framed flax warehouse of 1805 at the Ditherington Flax Mill, Shrewsbury. (Ironbridge Gorge Museum Archaeology Unit: Michael Worthington)

82 The most imposing of all factory warehouses, that at Manningham Mill, built in 1871–3. (Michael Stratton)

Merchants' palaces

Manningham apart, the finest Victorian textile warehouses were built away from the mills themselves. Merchants provided the essential links between most cloth manufacturers and their customers, and many opted to show their wares in private surroundings of increasing opulence rather than in public markets. Palazzo-style warehouses were built in Manchester from the 1840s, with large windows, surrounded by overscaled rusticated quoins and projecting cornices. While early examples could be compared with the clubs of Pall Mall, some were more akin to palaces:

'structures fit for kings which many monarchs might well envy'.

Distinctive warehouse quarters developed in most of the principal English textile cities in the mid-nineteenth century. The Lace Market district of Nottingham grew up around St Mary's Church, at first in adapted houses and then in purpose-built warehouses (83). Government reports indicate that Nottingham's warehouses were the commercial focus of the lace trade but that they also accommodated manufacturing processes. They were used for the 'dressing' of lace whereby material was stiffened with starch prior to finishing, and for bleaching and dyeing. The warehouses had large open floor areas, up to 75m (246ft) long, to allow lace to be spread out at full length to dry

83 Part of the Lace Market in Nottingham, designed by
T. C. Hine in 1853–5. The warehouse on the south side,
with its entrance flanked by bow windows, was
constructed for the firm of T. I. Birkin. That on the
southern corner belonged to the German firm of Jacoby.
(RCHME)

on wide frames. Other parts of the warehouse would be used for workers to remove or join surplus threads. The largest warehouses built in the 1850s were steam-heated and lit by gas. Many had top floors with long continuous rows of windows, lighting attics which were used for mending and hand finishing. Thomas Hine was responsible for the most impressive structures. He laid out the curving Broadway and designed its warehouses. His *tour de force* adorns nearby Stoney Street. Messrs Adams and Page's Warehouse was built in 1854–5 on an Elizabethan-style 'E'-plan. It rises to five storeys and incorporated facilities for machining and packaging lace as well as a library and a chapel, the latter being expressed externally by a group of traceried windows set in a projecting bay.

Little Germany

Growth in demand for lustre fabrics stimulated investment in warehouses in Bradford from around 1850. The progenitor was the Milligan, Forbes Warehouse built in 1851–2 to the design of Andrew & DeLauney in Peel Square. Its magnificent palazzo-style frontage demonstrates the effectiveness of an Italianate Renaissance style in evoking connotations of the residences of Florentine wool merchants. It also provided larger window openings than was possible with a Gothic elevation. Several warehouse precincts developed in Bradford. The most impressive is Little Germany, north-east of the city centre. Narrow streets were laid out on fields in 1856, and became chasm-like as they were lined with five-storey warehouses. Little Germany developed in a piecemeal manner, most rapidly in the years 1860–75, its merchants handling worsteds, mohairs and silks made in and around Bradford as well as blankets and carpets made in other West Riding towns.

The warehouses of Little Germany share common functions and elements. Large gateways gave access to internal yards, which were sometimes covered, ensuring that new goods were hidden from competitors' eyes. Cloth would be inspected and often dispatched

to a dyehouse, before returning for further scrutiny, probably in a top-lit attic. Hydraulic presses for packing were located at ground-floor level. Other machines, often steam-powered, rolled, folded and measured the cloth. Power-operated hoists were in use in Bradford by 1850. Hydraulic systems gained a brief vogue from the 1870s but electricity was systematically adopted from 1896. Customers entered through grand doorways to ornate entrance halls, lit by gas and later electricity, before being led up ornate staircases to the showcases. The most important room in an export warehouse was the counting-house on the first floor.

Many of the warehouses were designed and built as speculative ventures but the most striking examples were built as advertisements for particular firms. The dramatic atmosphere of Little Germany can be best appreciated in Burnett Street, where the warehouses De Vere House of 1871 and Law, Russell & Co. of 1874, both designed by Lockwood & Mawson, architects of Saltaire Mill, are set on either side of the road. The grand entrances, the first flanked by twin Corinthian columns and the latter topped by a carved eagle, both face down to the Leeds Road (**84**).

Manchester warehouses

Textile-warehouse design reached a grand finale in Manchester. New steel-framed buildings, faced with granite and terracotta, were built from the 1890s in Whitworth Street to handle the soaring output of the Lancashire cotton mills. Lloyds Packing Warehouses introduced the concept of 'a complete service of making up and packing facilities' provided by the specialist landlord packer who dispatched the goods on behalf of the shipping merchants. The company commissioned Harry S. Fairhurst to design a series of warehouses, commencing in 1899 and culminating with India House of 1905–6, Lancaster House with its soaring wedding-cake corner tower of 1907–9 (**85**), and Bridgewater House of 1912. These dramatic French Baroque structures, grouped at the western end of

84 Details of two of the finest warehouses in Little Germany: on the left De Vere House, of 1871, and on the right Law, Russell & Co., of 1874, both designed by Lockwood & Mawson. (Michael Stratton)

Whitworth Street, were designed to maximize internal light levels and to provide space for individual offices and warehouses, which could be partitioned by movable screens. Lorries could drive straight through the buildings, goods being unloaded by swinging cranes.

Twentieth-century storage

The most impressive multi-storey warehouse of the inter-war period, the base-stores at Fort Dunlop, can be studied from the M6 motorway near Birmingham's Spaghetti Junction. This seven-storey-plus-basement red brick structure, with no less than forty-four bays of deep windows, looks like a Lancashire cotton mill, and it is unsurprising that it was designed by an architect from Oldham, Sidney Gott, working with W. Gubbings of Birmingham. The stores,

completed in 1925, have a steel frame encased in concrete and supporting concrete floors. A glazed canopy at ground-floor level gave protection to the receiving and dispatch areas.

A revolution in materials handling led to the abandonment of city-centre warehouses for sprawling single-storey sheds located near to road junctions. Conveyors, fork-lift trucks and palletization made a new type of layout more practicable – a narrow plan reduced the distance between the taking-in and dispatch, but a long length allowed different materials and products to be allocated to different aisles. With bulk-handling even the distinctive warehouse feature of the raised floor, designed to line up with a tailboard or the interior of a railway wagon, was redundant. A wide spacing of columns became more critical. By the mid-1960s primitive forms of computer-controlled stacking justified the provision of greater ceiling heights, while the subsequent introduction of load-hauling or carrying robotugs, automatically following a trace wire in the floor, dictated the

85 The faience-clad exterior of Lancaster House, Whitworth Street, Manchester, by H. S. Fairhurst & Son, 1907–9: one of a group of cotton warehouses built in this part of the city in the early twentieth century. (Michael Stratton)

provision of wide gangways laid out on a circuit. Buffer stores in high stacks served by robots have replaced the multi-storey warehouse and the hoist, jigger and wheelbarrow. While Victorian warehouses often employed many workers and had to provide good lighting for the inspection of goods, modern stores are likely to be eerily deserted and lit night and day by fluorescent tubes. Most fundamentally the whole concept of storing raw materials, components and finished goods is not considered as a sign of commercial strength. In an age of containerization and just-in-time delivery schedules, the warehouse has come to be associated with inefficiency and with accumulations of unwanted goods.

8
Twentieth-century models

Most Victorian factories reflected the down-to-earth attitudes of their owners. Grimy exteriors and dimly lit, congested workshops were seen as the price that had to be paid for prosperity and profits. Belching chimneys symbolized a full order book rather than environmental irresponsibility, and a cramped urban location ensured proximity to workers and potential customers, as well as access to a local gas supply. A foundry, brassworks or pottery could be made to stand out from grimy terraces by highlighting the showroom, entrance archway and chimney with polished stone, glazed brick or tile.

A successful factory owner could retreat to a mansion in an exclusive suburb or silvan countryside. A worker had to live within walking, or later tram-riding, distance of the factory. Working conditions changed only slowly during the nineteenth century, except where reformist employers saw a link between working and living conditions and the morale and performance of the labour-force.

The rural ideal

From the mid-eighteenth century, some textile mills were established in the countryside, partly because their owners sought flowing water for power and clean water for dyeing, but also because a rural environment was likely to be free from machine-breaking Luddites, and to offer better opportunities for social control and the promotion of religious values.

In 1850 Titus Salt, a prosperous Bradford worsted manufacturer, decided to buy land in Airedale for a carefully planned mill and town, with the paternalistic aim of nurturing 'a population of well-paid, contented, happy operatives'. Saltaire, as it was less than modestly called (see **colour plate 8**), developed over the next twenty years to become a complete community. Visitors to this immaculately conserved model settlement are impressed by the way in which Salt and his designers, Lockwood & Mawson, used architecture to define a precise hierarchy of status and to impose its founder's values of hard work and self-help. The regimented grid layout of cobbled streets is lined by rows of Italianate terraces and houses – those for overlookers and managers having more rooms and ornamentation. The houses are overshadowed by the communal buildings – including an Institute and the Congregational church – but above all by the huge factory, described in 1853 as a 'model mill'.

The factory lost its focal status in the next generation of model settlements; it was demoted to a site on the edge of a village oriented primarily around communal buildings or open spaces. The manufactured products that funded Bournville, Port Sunlight and New Earswick – whether chocolate or soap – were best made in more openly planned works. At the same time well-read industrialists were wary of presenting their factories as assertions of wealth at a time when critics were writing of them as agents of economic and social divisiveness. William Morris was one of the commentators who railed against the 'tyranny' of 'bewildering factories'.

While Morris suggested the alternative of rural industrial colleges where work could be varied and machinery would play a subservient role, reformist captains of commerce sought to refine and even reinforce the discipline of mass production by locating their factories away from the squalor and temptations of the city in the more controlled setting of a tree-lined village. Budgett Meakin, who lectured on 'Industrial Betterment', gave a strictly commercial justification for model settlements; by 1905 he could refer to many companies in Britain and North America, that had successfully 'transplanted' to sparsely populated suburbs.

The celebrated examples – Bournville in Birmingham, and Port Sunlight in Birkenhead – can be visited by train; their stations signify the historic importance of rail links for bringing in workers and dispatching finished products. George Cadbury constructed a simple, single-storey Bournville works in 1878–9. Even with subsequent extensions the most striking feature remains the sports field with its Tudor-style pavilion. The factory at Port Sunlight was completed a decade later to designs by William Owen and consisted of two major blocks, each combining single-storey sheds and three-storey ranges, with the separate and smelly oil mills, alkali plant and glycerine works set close to the docks, well away from the village.

Cadbury's works was called a 'Factory in a Garden'. The first company houses were in an unremarkable utilitarian style, but from 1894 the village was given a rustic flavour, with curving roads, wide tree-bedecked verges, and a variety of architecture designed by W. Alexander Harvey. He used a deliberately limited range of bricks and tiles, with some half-timbering which gained credibility by the re-erection of two medieval houses close to the green and its rest-house. William Hesketh Lever, inventor of

Sunlight Soap, spread the commissions for his housing among many established architects. They worked within a succession of plans, the last of which was highly formal, with an art gallery at the end of a boulevard as its focus. Houses were designed in a dramatic medley of styles, ranging from French Gothic to half-timber work in the Cheshire vernacular, and utilizing expensive building materials, including Ruabon bricks, terracotta and moulded plaster (**colour plate 11**).

Some model settlements included facilities for eating and recreation away from the temptations of alcohol. At Port Sunlight residents decided in a poll to seek a licence for the 'temperance hotel' that Lever had provided. Cleanliness was nurtured through the provision of bath-houses.

Day-light factories

Model settlements were promoted with the slogan 'Welfare Pays', on the grounds that good living and working conditions contributed towards a healthy and loyal labour-force. Reformers introduced baths and canteens while managers retained traditional approaches to the organization of production and factory design. Historians have observed in the United States the source of the radical changes imported just before and during World War I that revolutionized the form of the British factory (**86**).

Around 1900 manufacturers in the United States were faced with an abundance of raw materials but a shortage of skilled workers. American engineering journals saw a solution in greater mechanization and a tight division of labour controlled by powerful management. This ideology was propounded in articles written by Frederick Taylor from 1895, and was summarized in his book *The Principles of Scientific Management*, published in 1911. Managers were advised to use clipboards and stop-watches in time-and-motion studies to analyse production lines. Factory layout, tools and conveyor routes could then be reworked to achieve the best possible level of productivity.

86 A daylight factory for the manufacture of footwear, built in 1923 in Rockingham Road, Kettering, for William Timpson & Son. (Barrie Trinder)

Taylor's ideas had obvious value for the American car industry, as it evolved from craft workshops to mass production in huge factories. Detroit emerged as the capital of the car industry and it was here that *Scientific Management* set the agenda for the factories designed by Albert Kahn, and most significantly for Highland Park, commissioned by Henry Ford to assemble the Model T.

Kahn condemned traditional factories as 'eyesores' that had grown 'like topsy' without rationality. He urged industrialists to start afresh rather than to extend and adapt, planning the most efficient paths for components and adopting conveyor systems that had already proved their worth in mail-order and meat-packing warehouses. Good lighting and heating were essential. Kahn came to advocate high, multi-storey buildings as opposed to single-storey sheds, calculating that they were 15 per cent cheaper to build for a given floor space,

ensured natural ventilation and lighting, and made power transmission more efficient.

Julius Kahn, Albert's brother, developed a form of concrete construction, patented in 1903, in which reinforcing wire and angled bars created strong concrete pillars and beams. The three-dimensional grid supported concrete-slab floors and permitted deep, metal-framed windows, so reducing fire risks and avoiding the narrow openings associated with timber joists and brick walls. Albert Kahn used concrete in a series of daylight factories for motor-car manufacture in Detroit, including the Packard No. 10 factory of 1905 and Henry Ford's four-storey, 244m (800ft) long Highland Park, erected in 1908.

The daylight factory was soon introduced in Britain. A third brother, Moritz Kahn, arrived in London in 1905, took out British patents on the Kahn reinforcing bar and in 1907 established a European company, Truscon, to promote the use of reinforced concrete. Several British car manufacturers created miniature Highland Parks, continuing the enthusiasm of some pioneering motor-car manufacturers for multi-storey works. The earliest purpose-built car factory in England was built by Henry Dennis in the middle of Guildford, Surrey, in 1900–1 (87). In this compact, three-storey, brick-walled building, now known as the Rodboro Buildings, cars were transported up through the floors by a lift to be finished under roof lights before being lowered to the showroom. Over the next decade several further firms made the curious decision to build cars in high buildings and turned to Truscon for progressive concrete structures. The most bizarre is the huge three-storey Arrol Johnston factory erected in a field on the edge of Dumfries in 1912–13, after the firm's manager

87 Rodboro Buildings, Guildford, Surrey, which is probably the earliest surviving purpose-built car factory in England, completed in 1901 to the design of J. Lake for Dennis Bros. Ltd. It quickly proved to be too small for the needs of the firm, who transferred production elsewhere in 1905, but continued to use it for offices until 1919. It was subsequently a footwear factory and a confectionary warehouse, and has recently been refurbished. (Michael Stratton)

had made a pilgrimage to inspect the Kahn plants in Detroit.

Wartime models

There was good reason to give attention to progressive ideas in factory design in the Edwardian period. Industrialists were alarmed by Britain's declining share of world trade, while politicians fretted at the poor physical condition of many who had volunteered for service in the Boer War. During World War I the need to maximize production of munitions and the introduction of women into manufacturing focused attention on working conditions.

The Ministry of Munitions, established in 1915, introduced new standards for the provision of washrooms and canteens. It developed 4000 'controlled establishments', where armaments were made by private firms on instructions from the ministry. Companies were encouraged to apply for ministry funding for major extensions or new factories, on condition that welfare facilities were incorporated in the design.

These controlled establishments lacked architectural ornamentation, but set precedents for the more stylish works of the inter-war period. Their design reflected the reports of committees that pondered the link between welfare and scientific management. Production was planned in logical paths and attention was given to lighting and ventilation. Some were single-storey structures, with steel or wooden roof trusses. The North and West works erected by Austin in 1916, now part of the Rover complex at Longbridge, Birmingham, can be identified to the north of the company's railway sidings, on opposite sides of the Bristol Road (**88**). Both were built with huge machine shops (one of them 260m/853ft long), two-storey

88 The Mini body shop in the West works at Longbridge in 1991. The completed body shells will be taken by conveyor to the paint shop. The West works was completed in June 1917, and was first used for making artillery shells. It was laid out for motor-body manufacture after World War I. (Michael Stratton)

office ranges and huge canteens, one of which accommodated 4000 people.

Other works erected by Truscon resembled Kahn's American daylight factories. BSA's 183m (600ft) long works in Small Heath, Birmingham, was built in three ranges during 1914 with a chequerboard grid of concrete piers and large windows. A portion still stands near the south end of the appropriately named Armoury Road.

Anticipating a return to peacetime commerce, Moritz Kahn wrote a book in 1917 proclaiming the advantages of concrete and multi-storey daylight construction. He itemized the advantages of multi-storey over single-storey layouts – cheaper construction per square foot, more even lighting, better supervision of workers, and easier distribution of parts via high-speed lifts. The plans all incorporated catering, toilet and first-aid facilities.

An engineer and an architect

The cause of the model factory was most strongly advanced in the inter-war period by an

engineer, Owen Williams, and an architect, Thomas Wallis. Both gained experience by working with Truscon and on military projects. Owen Williams appreciated concrete for its potential to create high, glass-clad buildings with wide open workspaces. He had little time for debates over questions of theory and style. His first daylight factory was designed in 1912, while working for Truscon. The machine shop for the Gramophone Company was set in the middle of a narrow complex located between the canal and the railway at Hayes, Middlesex. Its severe elevation – a grid of twelve bays across and six storeys high – was relieved only by a water tower perched at one end and letters publicizing 'His Master's Voice' to passengers on trains speeding to or from Paddington.

Williams honed his skills during World War I designing concrete hulls for tugs and lighters ordered by the Admiralty. After setting up his own practice in 1919, he designed buildings that juxtaposed bold masses of concrete, often to form cantilever weights balancing long-span beams, with planes of sheer glass. His *tour de force* in daylight architecture was the Wet Processes Building erected for Boots at Nottingham in 1930–3 (**colour plate 12**). In the best traditions of reformist employers, the company decided to replace a jumble of old workshops set amid slums with a crisp, efficient works built on open fields. Their engineer, Hedley Jessop, urged the adoption of flow-production techniques and efficient bottling machinery that he had observed on study tours to the United States and Europe. Williams, acting as the consulting engineer, designed a 162m (531ft) long rectangular block that allowed the various processes to be arranged in a logical flow from the unloading dock for raw materials on one side, through manufacturing to bulk stores, hence to the packing hall and the dispatch bay on the other side. The building was planned around a basic module of 2.33m (7ft 8in), the width of the panes of glass. An exterior akin to a gigantic greenhouse screens an internal structure of mushroom-headed concrete

columns, the flared-out capitals supporting the concrete floors above. Generous lighting provided by the floor-to-ceiling windows is augmented by the circular glass lights set into the concrete roof over the central packing hall, light flooding down through light wells which are surrounded by galleries and linking bridges. Goods are still fed down shutes from the third storey to the packing lines. Every detail of the design reflected Williams's commitment to what a contemporary critic described as 'law and order in planning, construction and working'.

Thomas Wallis took a less purist approach to factory design, responding to the wishes of industrialists to use architecture to advertise their products. As an employee of the Office of Works before 1914 he had worked on munitions factories. Once established in private practice, he made an agreement with Truscon in 1916 and gained a succession of commissions. Wallis, Gilbert & Partners found a ready market among image-conscious firms making consumer goods and designed about a hundred factory buildings during the inter-war period (see **90** and **colour plate 14**).

Some of Wallis's early designs relate closely to Kahn's American factories, being laid out on an almost standardized three-dimensional grid of columns, bays and windows, but, like Moritz Kahn, he appreciated the potential of decoration to 'redeem an otherwise dull building' and to make architecture a means of advertising and fostering staff morale. Simple Classical motifs – such as pilasters and cornices – were used in 1920 to adorn the office block of the Witton Engineering Works, Birmingham, a complex that can be observed from Spaghetti Junction. In 1926–8, inspired by the discovery of Tutankhamun's tomb, Wallis incorporated Egyptian motifs on the main elevation of the Wrigley Chewing Gum factory at Wembley, which fronts the main line out of Euston.

Wallis, Gilbert & Partners designed further multi-storey factories, especially for firms involved in precision manufacture. One of the most impressive groupings of their mammoth industrial structures was erected around Williams's machine shop at Hayes following the merger in 1931 that created EMI (Electrical & Musical Industries). For most types of industry they rejected two of the key features of the daylight factory – a concrete structure and multi-storey layout – in favour of steel construction and single-storey sheds.

By-pass factories: the Great West Road

During the inter-war period the model factory gave way to more pragmatically conceived works located alongside trunk roads, especially the by-passes built to speed access to the centre of London. Advocates of the 'Modern Movement' had given an exalted status to the factory, as a building type which reflected the energy and inventiveness of the age, and which could relate to the machine aesthetic expounded by the German training school known as the Bauhaus. They had cultivated an ideal, a purely 'functionalist' architecture, arising directly from the accommodation of particular processes and the adoption of modern forms of construction. Most industrialists thought in more down-to-earth terms, differentiating between the fundamental requirements of accommodating specific processes at modest cost, and the option of creating striking and colourful reception areas and entrances.

The principle of the by-pass factory was that the public and the work-force would focus their attention on an impressive two-storey office frontage with a dramatic central entrance, permitting the manufacturing area to the rear to be of single- or multi-storey construction, according to the dictates of the process and the site. Since the front would be clad in brick, stone, tile or render and the rear elevations were largely unseen, it made little visual difference whether the internal frame was of concrete or steel.

By-pass factories were dependent on road transport for the receipt and dispatch of goods, while many were engaged in producing tyres, windscreen wipers and other components for motor vehicles. It is unsurprising that their form derives from several prestigious car factories built in the first years of the twentieth century. Between 1903 and 1908 Clement-Talbot, Sheffield-Simplex, Argyll and Humber all built factories with palatial office blocks fronting single-storey production sheds. The pioneering example, the Clement-Talbot works, stands in excellent condition in Barlby Road, North Kensington, London (**colour plate 13**). The office block looks like a minor country house, with its cladding of brick and Portland stone, although the underlying structure is an early example of reinforced concrete. Potential customers left their horse carriages under a *porte-cochère* before inspecting cars displayed on a marble floor under a vaulted ceiling. The factory proper received no such ornament and consisted of a large, undivided area of north-lit sheds.

Two decades later this form of factory proved ideal for firms making light, consumer goods on the urban fringe, where land was cheap and plentiful, and mains electricity was available for lighting and power. A major impetus for investment came when successful American firms decided to set up in England in response to the imposition of a 33.3 per cent import duty in 1932. They viewed architecture as an important element in their marketing as well as part of their management systems, to inspire loyalty among the work-force and elevating the status of those managers who were allowed to use the formal, main entrance.

New arterial roads provided ideal settings for such image-conscious factories. Fourteen schemes, providing 190 miles (306km) of trunk roads, were built on the edge of London by 1926. The Great West Road, laid out over farmland and orchards to by-pass Brentford High Street, was begun in 1920 and completed in 1925. Industrial development followed. Since the new factories were close to central London, most of the firms combined their offices and production facilities. Within a decade, the section of the Great West Road from the

Chiswick roundabout to Syon Lane had become the best showcase of by-pass factory architecture in Britain.

Wallis, Gilbert & Partners gained most of the commissions. Thomas Wallis had accepted the practical advantages of steel frames and single-storey sheds around 1925 and proved a master at producing to time and to budget flexible workspaces and prestigious, panelled offices with concert rooms and sports facilities as required. North-lit roofs proved ideal for areas devoted to manufacturing whereas cheaper wide-span 'A'-section roofs sufficed for warehousing. Boiler houses and noxious processes were located to the rear. Roof heights could be adjusted to accommodate specific types of machine. The office block was more likely to be steel-framed rather than concrete-framed; in either case it would be given a facing of render or brickwork.

The most famous example, the Firestone factory, is, sadly, one of the few to have been demolished. From 1928 to 1980 its exotic Egyptian façade, with flashes of ceramic detailing, outshone its later neighbours. The use of tile and larger blocks of faience could be justified by psychological studies which demonstrated the influence of colour on workers, muted tones being recommended for interiors, while brighter, jade green, orange and red could enliven external elevations. Reflecting its relatively early date, the Firestone factory had a hybrid structure – the office block and the multi-storey warehouse at the back of the site had concrete frames while the central, manufacturing section was a steel-framed, north-lit shed.

The Pyrene factory, built on the opposite side of the highway in 1930 to make fire extinguishers and car components, is now the most striking example of Wallis's work on the Great West Road. The tile-decorated entrance under the tall central tower is approached by a formal stairway, the effect being to emphasize the long, low proportions of the side wings. The structure of the office block is of steel encased in

concrete and rendered in 'Atlas White' cement. The works was given 'all the virtues of a modern factory' – call bells, fresh-air ventilation, drinking fountains and a canteen. The main assembly shop was a north-lit shed, though some processes such as plating and polishing were housed in the frontage block.

In some by-pass factories, production processes were housed in what appear to be office blocks. To exploit to the full the corner site at the junction of Syon Lane, Banister Fletcher designed a factory for Gillette Industries, built in 1936, which appears to be a huge office block (**89**). Dirty and noisy processes were banished to a single-storey, north-lit shed at the rear. The steel-framed, concrete-clad, brick-faced structure rises to a soaring clock-tower fit for a city hall.

Any excursion to the Great West Road should conclude with a visit to Western Avenue, in nearby Perivale, for an inspection of the finest surviving example of by-pass architecture – the Hoover factory (**90**). The electric suction cleaner was a symbol of a brighter, liberated age and when Hoover set up a selling and servicing facility for their Canadian-made machines they gave Wallis, Gilbert & Partners full architectural rein. The frontage block, built in 1932 to house maintenance and dispatch as well as clerical departments, was rendered in white cement, its jazzy modernistic style focusing on the flared decoration of the central door entrance and fanlight above, and on flickers of orange and black tiling (**colour plate 14**). While the later production areas have been cleared for a supermarket, the office and maintenance block and the canteen building with its curved glass and streamlined image have been carefully restored.

A more sober image for industry was adopted in the late 1930s, drawing upon the examples of W. M. Dudok in Hilversum, Holland, and Charles Holden's designs for the London Underground. Many industrial architects made extensive use of plain brickwork to generate simple cubic masses, any decorative effects being

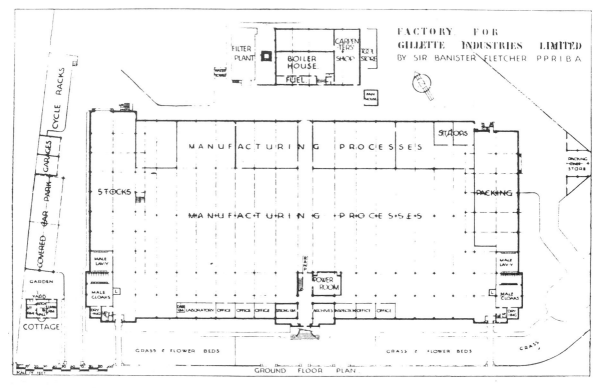

Within the plan image: FILTER PLANT · BOILER HOUSE · CARPENTERS' SHOP · FUEL · FACTORY FOR GILLETTE INDUSTRIES LIMITED BY SIR BANISTER FLETCHER PPRIBA · CYCLE RACKS · CAR PARK GARAGES · COVERED CAR PARK · MANUFACTURING PROCESSES · STORES · STOCKS · MANUFACTURING PROCESSES · PACKING · PACKING STORE · GARDEN · YARD · COTTAGE · MALE LAV'Y · MALE CLOAKS · POWER ROOM · MALE LAV'Y · MALE CLOAKS · LABORATORY · OFFICE · OFFICE · OFFICE · STRONG RM · ARCHIVES · INSPECTN OFFICE · OFFICE · GRASS & FLOWER BEDS · GRASS & FLOWER BEDS · GRASS · GROUND FLOOR PLAN

89 Ground-floor plan of the Gillette factory, London, designed by Sir Banister Fletcher and completed in 1936. (*Architectural Design & Construction*, VII, 1936)

restricted to a central, office entrance or the top of a tower.

This formula created a consistent image for the 'shadow' factories built from 1937 as part of the government's policy of rearmament. The Air Ministry paid for new plants to make aero-engine components under the management of well-established car producers. The production of components and engines was carefully co-ordinated, one factory 'shadowing' the production of another. Most were located in the West Midlands They share a common layout and structure, derived from car factories of the early 1930s, such as those of Ford at Dagenham. Production was housed under one or possibly two vast roofs, either north-lit or ridge-and-furrow in form, the lack of overhead line-shafting permitting wide bay widths and high clearances. These spaces, in some cases over half a mile long, have proved readily adaptable for the production of complete aircraft, cars and tractors as well as engines and other components. One of the least-altered examples is in Banner Lane, Coventry. It was built by Standard and is now used by Massey Ferguson for making tractors. The perfectly lit production hall now houses a variety of production lines, overhead conveyors, robots, buffer stores and fully automated machine-tool stations. Shadow factories have proved the most successful and adaptable of all Britain's industrial building types.

The industrial estate

Just as there are model factories, so there are model settings for factories. Saltaire, Port Sunlight and Bournville were the creation of mature but still-expanding enterprises. The traditional nursery of industrial enterprise was an existing building, a derelict workshop, an abandoned house, a railway arch. Imagination was required to envisage the creation of a landscape conducive to enterprise and salubrious for its work-force, where large and

90 A view taken in 1982 of the rear block and loading bay of the Hoover factory, Western Avenue, Perivale, developed from 1932 and designed by Wallis, Gilbert & Partners. Note the massive area of window provided to illuminate the main working areas. (RCHME)

small, mature and fledgling concerns could share common facilities.

The concept of the industrial estate has long antecedents. In 1656 the Swedish King Carl Gustaf laid out on a grid-plan twenty wooden smithy buildings, designed to attract skilled German migrants, which was the nucleus of the renowned engineering city of Eskilstuna. In post-Restoration England, Andrew Yarranton advocated the establishment of new settlements with diversified manufactures at nodal points in the transport system. Nevertheless the originator of the twentieth-century beliefs that manufacturing should be concentrated in zones separate from residential areas, and that factories should be mixed in size and products,

is usually considered to be Ebenezer Howard, whose book, *Tomorrow: A Peaceful Path to Real Reform* (from 1902, *Garden Cities of Tomorrow*), was published in 1899. Letchworth, founded in 1903, and Welwyn Garden City, established in 1919, embodied Howard's ideals, as did Harlow, Crawley, Milton Keynes and other towns built under the New Towns Act of 1946.

The concept of a planned estate where a variety of manufactures could flourish pre-dated the publication of Howard's book. The pioneer organizations in this, as in other aspects of consumer goods manufacture, were the co-operative societies. The Scottish Co-operative Wholesale Society established its main manufacturing centre at Shieldhall on Renfrew Road, Glasgow, from 1887, completing buildings for seventeen departments by 1918. Most of the buildings were in red and white brick. By 1909 the estate accommodated such varied manufactures as hosiery, coffee essence, brushes, tailoring, boots, confectionery and pickle, and common services were provided by a cooperage, a power station, dining-rooms and a range of stables. Work commenced on the English equivalent, at Pelaw, Co. Durham, on May Day 1902. By 1909 five ranges of two- and three-storey top-lit buildings had been erected, making brushes, coffee and polish, among other products.

The more widely acknowledged prototype of industrial estates in Britain was Trafford Park (91), developed from 1896 at the initiative of Marshall Stevens, managing director of the Manchester Ship Canal, which bordered the site and had opened two years earlier, giving ocean-going ships access to the metropolis of the Lancashire cotton industry. Trafford Park provided a range of new industries which sustained Manchester's economy through much of the twentieth century. Railway and tramway communications, hydraulic and electric power

were provided for companies which took space on the estate. Terraced housing on a grid-plan was constructed for some employees, but Trafford Park depended on electric tramways, and most workers arrived on 'gondolas of the people'. Employment on the estate reached a peak of 75,000 towards the end of World War II. Many of the buildings on the estate were factories and warehouses of no special architectural distinction, constructed from

91 An aerial view of Trafford Park, highlighting the engineering works established by George Westinghouse in 1900, which was later operated by Metropolitan Vickers, at its maximum extent *c.* 1945. The main part of the works is enclosed within a bend of the Bridgewater Canal. In the background are the Manchester Ship Canal and Salford Docks. In the centre are the rows of terraced housing which accommodated a small portion of the labour-force employed at Trafford Park. (Ironbridge Gorge Museum Trust)

locally made bricks, with the lightweight forms of steel construction conventional in the early years of the twentieth century. Trafford Park was particularly significant as the point at which twentieth-century American technology was transferred to Britain.

Henry Ford opened his first factory in England in Trafford Park on 23 October 1911, and within three years was using flow-production methods. In 1931 the company moved to Dagenham. The main production sheds at Trafford Park have been demolished, but some subsidiary buildings remain, most of them used by a timber merchant. Several large roller flour mills were constructed on the banks of the Ship Canal, around an American-designed grain elevator. The Owens Bottle Machine Co. from Toledo, Ohio, for whom Michael Joseph Owens had patented the machine which made possible the mass production of bottles, opened a factory in Trafford Park in 1906. In 1913 Moritz Kahn's Truscon company opened a depot providing materials from which reinforced concrete buildings could be constructed. The most spectacular transatlantic presence on the estate is the huge factory built by George Westinghouse in 1901–3 and described in Chapter 6 (see **72**). At its peak, at the end of World War II, the factory employed 26,000 workers. The main shops, together with the American-style office block, remain as central points in the Trafford Park landscape, which can readily be viewed from the M63 on the western side of Manchester.

During the 1920s the munitions factories and depots established around London during World War I to supply the armies fighting on the Western Front were the stimulus which made the western and north-western suburbs of the capital one of the principal industrial regions of Britain. The Hyde at Colindale, and Park Royal, the greatest concentration of manufacturing activity in southern England where over 30,000 people were employed in 1952, both grew up around munitions factories, but the development which epitomized industry

in the inter-war period was the Slough Trading Estate. Slough's growth stimulated John Betjeman's grotesque lines:

Come, friendly bombs, and fall on Slough
It isn't fit for humans now

The estate was built on a 270ha (668-acre) farm, taken over in 1918 as a base for a motorized offensive on the Western Front planned for 1919. Thousands of vehicles on the site were sold off by a company experienced in the motor trade, which by the autumn of 1920 had come to appreciate the development potential of the land, and had leased several plots for industrial use. The company took the name of Slough Estates Ltd. The last military vehicles were sold in 1925, and the remainder of the site was divided into plots for factories. The company installed railway, roads, water, gas, steam and electric-power supplies. Plots for factories were laid out along formal avenues, some lined with grass verges. Many of the best-known consumer products of the inter-war period were made at Slough: O-Cedar mops, St Martins jam, Aspro, Mars Bars, Chappie dog food and Black & Decker tools, but there were also significant engineering factories, among them the Citroën car plant, opened in 1925 and closed in 1966, and for a time 'the largest factory under one roof' in Britain. In economic terms, Slough was successful, giving employment to 23,000 people by 1939.

The concept of the industrial estate came to be accepted in the public sector during the 1930s. The Special Areas (Amendment) Act of 1937, a measure intended to reduce unemployment, encouraged the development of estates where companies establishing factories could enjoy freedom from rates and certain taxes for up to five years. The first such estates were in the Team valley in County Durham, at Treforest in South Wales and North Hillington in Glasgow, and others were in the course of development by 1939. The first factories were of modular construction, those at Treforest being of 6000, 12,000 or 24,000sq ft (c. 557, 1114 or 2228sq m). Companies have added ornate administrative buildings on to the frontages of the unadorned sheds, and it is now difficult to recognize the original structures. The Team Valley Trading Estate developed from north to south, and its buildings reflect the changing nature of post-war factories. One of the first was erected by the Huwood Mining Machinery Co. Its pale buff brick walls contrast with the metal cladding and polychromatic brick of more modern works manufacturing consumer goods.

After World War II the industrial zone or trading estate became a commonplace of planning policy in towns like Telford and Washington, built under the New Towns Act of 1946. Similar estates have been created on the edges of towns, on old military bases and in areas vacated by heavy industry in every part of Britain. A characteristic industrial estate of the late twentieth century, such as that to the east of the University of Aston, is likely to be called a business park or, if it is near a university, a science park, and to consist of brightly coloured but anonymous, unfenestrated metal-clad sheds, standing amid neatly cultivated lawns and parking lots for BMWs and Jaguars. Such an estate has a pedigree which extends back for three centuries.

9
Conclusions: evolution and adaptation

Manufacturing has been one of the dominant human activities over the last two centuries. Millions of people work in factories whose form is derived from precedents established during the British Industrial Revolution. To develop an understanding of the development of factory buildings is therefore to gain insights into significant aspects of modern civilization and culture.

Factories, like any other source of historical evidence, can continually reveal new insights when studied afresh. To see an industrial building at a different time of day, or in different company, can stimulate new questions, and in the study of factories – as in the study of henge monuments, medieval cathedrals or Renaissance palaces – understanding is advanced by the incisiveness and appropriateness of questions, rather than by the volume of data which can be accumulated. We have discussed in this book some of the issues about buildings which are currently on the agenda of thinking industrial archaeologists. We are aware that as the discipline progresses the agenda will change.

It is easy to assert that factories were designed to accommodate particular technological systems. Some certainly were. The Stotts' spinning mills (see Chapter 4) were intended to accommodate exact numbers of mules or ring spinning frames, with appropriate ranges of devils, carding frames, roving frames and doublers. Purpose-built electric power stations were designed for specific numbers of generating sets with matching boilers or water turbines. But to see factories only as buildings which were intended to house machines is to take a one-dimensional and unhistorical view. All factories accommodated people, even if in an inhumane fashion. Furthermore relatively few industrial buildings were used in the same way for long periods of time. Most were adapted to deploy succeeding generations of machines, and new concepts of organizing production and accommodating workers. James Nasmyth embarked on his career as a maker of machines in the 1830s by leasing space in a tenemented multi-storey cotton mill in Dale Street, Manchester (see **62**). Staverton Mill of 1824, the flagship of the Wiltshire woollen industry, was adapted in 1897–8 for the production of condensed milk (see **47**). Comparative research has enabled the development of a hypothesis to explain how machines in the Ditherington Flax Mill were deployed when it was erected in the 1790s (see Chapter 5), but within a generation the building was used in different ways (**92**).

Adaptable space might seem a concept which belongs to the late twentieth century, an era of rapid technological development, when some are obsessed with the 'management of change'. The architect of the H. J. Heinz food factory at Kitt Green near Wigan, completed in 1957, contrasted it with the first purpose-built Heinz factory in Britain which had opened in north London in 1925. The latter was 'designed

92 The Ditherington Flax Mill, Shrewsbury, the first iron-framed factory, and an example of how industrial buildings have been adapted over time. Built as a flax-spinning mill in 1796–7, it was gradually adapted as a specialist thread factory in the mid-nineteenth century, closed in 1886, and opened as a maltings c. 1900, which purpose it served until 1987, except for an interval as a military barracks during World War II. (Barrie Trinder)

tailor-made to the production requirements of the time', while the buildings at Kitt Green were 'so designed that they are complete functional units and aesthetically right from the start: and they must remain so at each expansion'. Continual adaptation to technological change seems a modern concept, and one which is given physical form in the multi-coloured sheds erected by speculative developers and government agencies on the business parks of the 1990s. Nevertheless it is a concept which has a long history. Recent research has shown that some early nineteenth-century textile mills in Manchester were designed to provide *room and power*, and to be used in any ways which the occupying entrepreneurs might find appropriate. North-lit sheds have been used to manufacture many

different products. The shadow factories of the late 1930s have proved some of the most useful industrial buildings in British history. It might therefore be argued that readily adaptable space rather than the capacity to accommodate a particular technology is the prime requirement of an industrial building. Constant technological change is a characteristic not just of the late twentieth century but of most forms of manufacture since the Industrial Revolution, and the successful buildings are those in which it can best be managed.

Power and the means of transmitting it to a multitude of machines may be seen as the essence of the factory as it evolved during the industrial revolution. There are instances of semi-religious devotion to prime movers. The opulent setting of an engine like that at Trencherfield Mill, Wigan (see **colour plate 5**), shows the esteem in which it was held. Yet it is misleading to see the prime mover as the necessary nucleus of a factory. Manufacturing often took place in large buildings before technology made possible the use of powered machines for particular processes. This might be done in order to achieve efficiency by concentrating a succession of processes in one place. It could be done in order to discipline the labour-force. Its purpose might be to enhance security. To explain how power was generated and distributed is a key task for an industrial archaeologist investigating a factory, but in some complexes the nucleus was not the prime mover.

Our understanding of industrial buildings increases as we see them in broader contexts. It is easy to be impressed by a building of architectural merit, but such a building may be only one element in a complex, which may have accumulated over time. In order to explain the original purpose or the function over time of the outstanding building, it is essential to understand its relationship with other component buildings, to see it in the architectural context of its region, and to compare it with buildings elsewhere designed to accommodate the same technology. Model factories and model industrial settlements such as Saltaire and Bournville should be seen not as typical or characteristic buildings of particular periods or regions – there are no factories *like* Stanley Mill or industrial settlements *like* Port Sunlight – but as subtle texts, which can be decoded to enhance our understanding of all factories or settlements.

The rich legacy of industrial monuments in England should not be regarded simply as a collection of shrines to a distant past when the nation was 'the workshop of the world'. Conserved steam engines and kilns, textile mills and warehouses which have been adapted to new uses, are, rather, a positive means of interpreting our history. Our understanding of the place of manufacturing within our society, whether during the Industrial Revolution or in the twentieth century, will only increase if it is subjected to new forms of analysis. Industrial buildings offer stimulating challenges to our thinking. This book has summarized some aspects of what has been learned about the industrial past during the four decades since Industrial Archaeology was named in print.

Some of the most significant structures of the Industrial Revolution period are presented to the public. It is possible to visit Richard Arkwright's Cromford Mill, to admire museum displays in Jesse Hartley's warehouse at Albert Dock, Liverpool, or to walk across the Iron Bridge. Some notable products of the period are held in museums: pottery at the City Museum, Stoke-on-Trent, locomotives at the National Railway Museum, York, machine tools at the Science Museum, London. Other important factories, including some of the twentieth century, have been adapted to new uses. It is possible to buy David Hockney prints in Saltaire Mill, or groceries from the Hoover building in Perivale. Yet the industrial past can often be sensed most vividly in less-celebrated landscapes, in the curious *mélange* of footwear factories and domestic workshops on the northern side of Kettering, or amid the bustle of trucks and vans serving the late twentieth-century enterprises of Trafford Park or Slough. Industrial buildings are above all a reflection of human endeavour, and we understand their significance as we come to appreciate the nature and significance of that activity.

Glossary

auger A hollow tube with a rotating screw mechanism, used for moving grain between floors at flour mills, and for the conveyance of similar bulk materials at other factories.

blast furnace A furnace in the form of a shaft, charged with iron ore, fuel and a flux, and blown with air, in which the ore is smelted to produce cast iron.

cast iron Iron with a significant carbon content (1.8–4.5 per cent) which can be cast in moulds, and is strong in compression but weak in tension.

concrete A mixture of sand and gravel or stone, bound together with lime or cement.

cone A conical brick structure, built around a glass kiln or kilns, which serves to increase the draught; sometimes called an English Glass Cone.

daylight factory A type of multi-storey factory developed in the United States in the early twentieth century, characterized by having large windows and a concrete frame.

extrusion A process in which a material in a pliable state is forced through a die, which is widely used in the ceramic, plastic and aluminium industries.

flax A fibre derived from the stem of the flax plant, used to make linen.

fulling mill A machine in which woollen cloth is pounded with various substances, including water, urine, fuller's earth or soap, to achieve a controlled shrinkage of the fabric.

headstock The structure at the head of the shaft of a mine, carrying a pulley across which runs the rope from the shaft to the winding engine, traditionally of wood, but in the twentieth century of steel or concrete.

Hoffman kiln A kiln, circular or oval in plan, originally developed by Friedrich Hoffman in Austria in 1856, and used for firing ceramic wares and burning lime.

modernist architecture A term applied to some twentieth-century buildings, dating from the period c. 1910 to c. 1970, characterized by their simple outlines and lack of ornamentation.

north-lit shed A factory building with saw-tooth pattern, north-facing roof lines set almost vertically and filled with glass, with the south-facing slopes solid, which ensured soft internal lighting, free from glare.

pugmill A machine with rotating metal blades used to break down clay for pressing or extrusion.

steel An alloy of iron and other elements, with a carbon content of between 0.5 and 1.3 per cent, made on a large scale which enabled its use in construction from the 1850s.

truss A framework of wooden or metal beams or bars supporting a roof or bridge.

wrought iron A commercially pure form of iron, fibrous in texture and strong in tension.

Further reading

General works

Cossons, N., *The BP Book of Industrial Archaeology* (3rd edn, Newton Abbot: David & Charles 1993)

Falconer, K., *Guide to England's Industrial Heritage* (London: Batsford 1980)

Trinder, B., *The Making of the Industrial Landscape* (London: Dent 1982)

Trinder, B., *The Blackwell Encyclopedia of Industrial* Archaeology (Oxford: Blackwell 1992)

Accommodating people

Calladine, A. and Fricker, J., *East Cheshire Textile Mills* (London: Royal Commission on the Historical Monuments of England 1993)

Giles, C. and Goodall, I. H., *Yorkshire Textile Mills* (London: HMSO for Royal Commission on the Historical Monuments of England 1992)

Smith, W. J., *Saddleworth Buildings: A Guide to the Vernacular Architecture of the Parish of Saddleworth in the Pennines* (Saddleworth: Saddleworth Historical Society 1987)

Tann, J., *The Development of the Factory* (London: Cornmarket 1970)

Williams, M., *Cotton Mills in Greater Manchester* (Preston: Carnegie, for the Royal Commission on the Historical Monuments of England 1992)

Accommodating power

Hunter, L. C., *Water Power: A History of Industrial Power in the United States 1780–1830*, 2 vols (Charlottesville, VA: University Press of Virginia 1979)

Hunter, L. C. and Bryant, L., *A History of Industrial Power in the United States 1780–1830, vol III, The Transmission of Power* (Cambridge, MA: MIT Press 1991)

Jarvis, A., *Hydraulic Machines* (Princes Risborough: Shire Publications 1985)

The changing complex

Baker, D., *Potworks: The Industrial Architecture of the Staffordshire Potteries* (London: Royal Commission on the Historical Monuments of England 1991)

Collins, P. and Stratton, M., *British Car Factories from 1896* (Godmanstone: Veloce 1993)

Function or fashion?

Binney, M., Hamm, M. and Föhl, A., *Great Railway Stations of Europe* (London: Thames & Hudson 1984)

Richards, J. M., *The Functional Tradition in Early Industrial Buildings* (London: Architectural Press 1958)

Simmons, J., *St Pancras Station* (London: Allen & Unwin 1968)

Watson, M., *Jute and Flax Mills in Dundee* (Tayport: Hutton 1990)

Strength, span and security

Collins, P., *Concrete: The Vision of a New Architecture* (London: Faber & Faber 1959)

Yarranton, A., *England's Improvement by Sea and Land* (London: Everingham 1677)

Making machines

Cantrell, J. A., *James Nasmyth and the Bridgewater Foundry: A Study of Entrepreneurship in the Early Engineering Industry* (Manchester: Chetham Society 1984)

Cleere, H. and Crossley, D., *The Iron Industry of the Weald* (Leicester: Leicester University Press 1985)

Falconer, K. and Cattel, J., *Swindon: Legacy of a Railway Town* (Swindon: Royal Commission on the Historical Monuments of England 1995)

Peck, A. S., *The Great Western at Swindon Works* (Poole: Oxford Publishing Co. 1983)

Steeds, W., *A History of Machine Tools 1700–1910* (Oxford: Clarendon Press 1969)

More than safe storage: the warehouse

Coad, J. G., *The Royal Dockyards 1690–1850* (Aldershot: Scolar 1989)

Jackson, G., *The History and Archaeology of Ports* (Tadworth: World's Work 1983)

Twentieth-century models

Hall, P., *The Industries of London* (London: Heinemann 1962)

Meakin, B., *Model Factories and Villages: Ideal Conditions of Labour and Housing* (London: Fisher Unwin 1905)

Journals

Journals published in Britain which discuss some of the issues raised in the book include *Construction History*, *Industrial Archaeology Review*, *Textile History* and the *Transactions of the Newcomen Society*. North American publications include *Industrial Archeology*, *Material History Review* and *Technology & Culture*.

Index of places

(Page numbers in **bold** refer to illustrations)

Subject index

This classification is based on that used in
Trinder, B. *The Blackwell Encyclopedia of
Industrial Archaeology* (Oxford: Blackwell,
1992), pp. 861–72

CHEMICALS
 Explosives, 33, **35**, 48–9, **48**
 Soap, 106–7

CIVIL ENGINEERING
 Concrete construction, **32**, 68–73, **71**, **73**,
  108–9
 Fireproof construction, 66–7, 93
 Iron-framing, 65–8, **66**, **68**, **99**
 Steel-framing, **32**, 68–9, **69**, 98–9, **98**

FACTORIES
 Architectural styles, 50–63
 By-pass factory, 112–13

Component structures, 33
Courtyard layout, 33–7, 42, 44–5, 83
Daylight factory, 20, 107–8, 122
Demarcation, 25
Dining facilities, 23–4, 107–9
Educational facilities, 24
Heating, 21–2, 32, 108
Lighting, 20, 108, 110
North-lit shed, 20, **36**, 52, 68–9, 87,
 113, 120, 122
Sanitary facilities, 22
Shadow factory, 49, 114, 120
Washing facilities, 22, 38, 62, 107,
 109

INDUSTRIAL COMMUNITIES
 Domestic manufactures, 13–20
 Model communities, 11, 106–7,
  115

IRON
 Blast furnaces, 24, 51–2, 59, 75–6, 122
 Steelmaking, 68–9

MANUFACTURING INDUSTRY
 Bricks, 37, 39, 40–2, **43**, 78
 Ceramics, 10, 42–4, **45**, 53
 Drugs, 111
 Food, 25, 61
 Footwear, 13, 61–2
 Glass, 37, **37**, **38**, 117
 Leather, 62, 63, **93**
 Saw mills, 64
 Tobacco, **93**, **94**, 95

MECHANICAL ENGINEERING
 Agriculture machinery, 84
 Aircraft, 10, 47–9, **53**
 Cranes, 76, 82–3, 96

Index of names and companies

The Authors

Dr Michael Stratton (left) and Dr Barrie Trinder (right) worked together for fifteen years at the Ironbridge Institute, developing Masters programmes in Industrial Archaeology and Heritage Management, compiling the first international encyclopaedia of Industrial Archaeology and undertaking a wide range of consultancy projects.

Michael Stratton is now Lecturer in Conservation Studies at the University of York and has recently published on aircraft factories, the railway heritage and twentieth-century architecture. Barrie Trinder is Senior Lecturer in Industrial Archaeology at Nene College. He is the author of recent publications on the Industrial Archaeology of Shropshire and on World Heritage Sites. Both have travelled widely, studying industrial conservation in Europe and North America.

'One of the great classic series of British archaeology.' *Current Archaeology*

This volume is part of a major series, jointly conceived for English Heritage and Batsford, under the general editorship of Dr Stephen Johnson at English Heritage.

Titles in the series:

Sites
Avebury Caroline Malone
Danebury Barry Cunliffe
Dover Castle Jonathan Coad
Flag Fen: Prehistoric Fenland Centre Francis Pryor
Fountains Abbey Glyn Coppack
Glastonbury Philip Rahtz
Hadrian's Wall Stephen Johnson
Housesteads James Crow
Ironbridge Gorge Catherine Clark
Lindisfarne Deirdre O'Sullivan and Robert Young
Maiden Castle Niall M. Sharples
Roman Bath Barry Cunliffe
Roman London Gustav Milne
Roman York Patrick Ottaway
Stonehenge Julian Richards
Tintagel Charles Thomas
The Tower of London Geoffrey Parnell
Viking Age York Richard Hall
Wharram Percy: Deserted Medieval Village Maurice Beresford and John Hurst
Forthcoming
St Augustine's Abbey Richard Gem et al.

Periods
Anglo-Saxon England Martin Welch
Bronze Age Britain Michael Parker Pearson
Industrial England Michael Stratton and Barrie Trinder
Iron Age Britain Barry Cunliffe
Roman Britain Martin Millett
Viking Age England Julian D. Richards
Forthcoming
Norman England Trevor Rowley
Stone Age Britain Nick Barton

Subjects
Abbeys and Priories Glyn Coppack
Canals Nigel Crowe
Castles Tom McNeill
Channel Defences Andrew Saunders
Church Archaeology Warwick Rodwell
Life in Roman Britain Joan Alcock
Prehistoric Settlements Robert Bewley
Roman Towns in Britain Guy de la Bédoyère
Roman Villas and the Countryside Guy de la Bédoyère
Shrines and Sacrifice Ann Woodward
Victorian Churches James Stevens Curl
Forthcoming
Roman Forts in Britain Paul Bidwell
Seaside Architecture Simon H. Adamson
Ships and Shipwrecks Peter Marsden

Towns
Canterbury Marjorie Lyle
Chester Peter Carrington
Durham Martin Roberts
Norwich Brian Ayers
Winchester Tom Beaumont James
York Richard Hall

Landscapes
Dartmoor Sandy Gerrard
The Peak District John Barnatt and Ken Smith
Forthcoming
The Cotswolds Timothy Darvill and Alan McWhirr
The Yorkshire Dales Robert White